KRIEGIE 7956

Lieutenant Gatewood's Journeys
September 10, 1944–April 29, 1945

KRIEGIE 7956

A WORLD WAR II BOMBARDIER'S
PURSUIT OF FREEDOM

By

Betty Jean Belkham Gatewood

as related to her by
former U.S. Army Air Corps 2nd Lt. Vernon L. "Gate" Gatewood

BURD STREET PRESS
SHIPPENSBURG, PENNSYLVANIA

Photographs and illustrations are from Vernon Gatewood's collection except as noted.

This Burd Street Press publication
was printed by
Beidel Printing House, Inc.
63 West Burd Street
Shippensburg, PA 17257-0708 USA

The acid-free paper used in this book meets the guidelines for permanence and durability of the Committee on Production Guidelines for Book Longevity of the Council on Library Resources.

For a complete list of available publications
please write
Burd Street Press
Division of White Mane Publishing Company, Inc.
P.O. Box 708
Shippensburg, PA 17257-0708 USA

Library of Congress Cataloging-in-Publication Data

Gatewood, Betty Jean Belkham, 1947-
    Kriegie 7956 : a World War II bombardier's pursuit of freedom / by Betty Jean Belkham Gatewood as related to her by Vernon L. Gatewood.
        p. cm.
    Includes bibliographical references (p.) and index.
    ISBN 1-57249-281-3 (alk. paper)
    1. Gatewood, Vernon L. 2. United States. Army Air Forces--Biography. 3. Bombardiers--United States--Biography. 4. World War, 1939-1945--Prisoners and prisons, German. 5. Prisoners of war--United States--Biography. I. Gatewood, Vernon L. II. Title

D805.G3 G375 2001
940.54'4973'092--dc21
[B]
                                                                2001037858

PRINTED IN THE UNITED STATES OF AMERICA

CONTENTS

ILLUSTRATIONS

Foreword

As an officer in the United States Air Force for 30 years, father of three, and son of a World War II B-17 pilot, I am concerned about how little my children and members of their generation know about World War II. Growing up I was in awe of the total commitment and sacrifice my parents and their friends and relatives made to our country during that period. Stories of my dad and his friends giving up their businesses to go to war, of gas rationing, and of women going to work abounded. I grew up knowing that in the forties my parents' apartment in New Jersey became a gathering place for those traveling to the front or returning from war, and my mom even published a small newsletter to keep friends aware of who had been by and where friends were stationed around the world.

Throughout my air force career I spent many, many hours studying the lessons of World War II during military courses at the U.S. Air Force Academy, Squadron Officers School, Air Command and Staff College, and Air War College. The lessons about the importance of having a strong military force, the decision of Great Britain to concentrate on building fighters rather than bombers in the thirties, and the United States' lack of a long-range fighter aircraft to escort its bombers were amongst those etched in my mind. I became interested in World War II and have read numerous books on the subject including ones about D-Day, Patton's dash across Europe, Von Manstein's battles in Russia, and the enormous destruction during the battle for Stalingrad. The two things that amaze me most about the war are both the total commitment and day-to-day sacrifice made by the folks at home in the U.S. and the monumental logistics efforts necessary on the part of every country to fight a war literally all over the world.

Of course, one of the major changes in the U.S. military resulting from World War II was the creation of a separate air force. Through the dedication of hundreds of thousands of men like Vernon Gatewood, the U.S. military learned that the speed, range, and flexibility of air power could be used more effectively if the air force were organized as a separate service the way it was in Great Britain. Thus, in 1947, the U.S. military was reorganized to make the army air corps a separate service called the U.S. Air Force. Using many of the lessons from World War II, it has evolved into the most effective air force in the world today.

I have learned a great deal about World War II, but, of course, no amount of book learning can take the place of being there. The next best thing to being there is hearing it from those who have been there, and that's why this work is so important. It's been apparent over the years that most folks who took part in World War II are reluctant to discuss it. When I was a child I asked my mom why my dad never talked about the war. She said that the people who were the closest to the fighting found it difficult to talk about. However, now that the war is in the distant past, we are in danger of losing the real story as it can only be told by those who lived it. That's why it is so vital for the quiet heroes of a passing generation like Vernon Gatewood's to tell their story. This war was so enormous, so costly, and so devastating in terms of human lives lost and suffering it caused that a war like it must never happen again. Hopefully this book can play a small, but pivotal role in educating new generations about the sacrifices necessary to preserve our freedoms and about why we should remain strong and appreciate our freedoms so we don't see the likes of World War II again.

Terry R. Silvester
Colonel, USAF (Retired)

PREFACE

The educational possibilities of this story came to me some years ago when I realized that some of the war era anecdotes from my father and mother-in-law were not only entertaining, but moving and compelling. Stories about their wedding, his Caterpillar Club membership, his hatred of snow, and his distaste for Jell-O should be shared. Then when my daughter was delving into family genealogy in Peggy Beck's third-grade class, I knew that this story had to be told so others could read it. Betsy learned a few, yet brief, stories about her grandparents then, but the veteran was a little reluctant to share, and the child was too young to understand the enormity of the situation. I jotted down some ideas, but other things took my time and the story never flowed.

Over the next few years of her adolescent development, I began to realize that Betsy was better able to understand the mature concepts such as those surrounding a World War II experience. Also, she was in third grade when I began the story and she no longer wanted to be "in print" as a youngster. I understood that perfectly. That's when we ditched the original first chapter and put her in Sue Simmons' high-school history class. Her more mature perspective now allows her to understand, be compassionate, and appreciate her grandfather's sacrifices for freedom. She can also better put his experiences into a world history perspective and be proud of his efforts to maintain our freedoms. The high-school viewpoint for telling the story seemed to work. Betsy understands World War II better now, and she has learned it in a personal way. These lessons are not forgotten. My hope is that Betsy will pick up the pursuit of freedom that her grandfather pursued so valiantly and by so doing, encourage others to document similar stories.

As a teacher, I have found that you must seize the teachable moment and run with it. At S. Gordon Stewart Middle School for the last three springs, local veterans of World War II, Korea, Vietnam, and the Gulf War are invited to school for a recognition ceremony that culminates several weeks of studying the last half of the 20th century. Under the expert direction of sixth-grade social studies teacher (and my former coworker/teaching buddy), Linda Petzke, our students study stories, wars, and veterans culminating in the "Heroes' Welcome." Stories are shared, presentations are made, experiences are honored. It is enthralling and of high interest for a middle-school student to hear a story in which the main character has faced deprivation, adversity, fear, sacrifice, and danger—and survived. I decided that my target audience was found. The historical groundwork had been laid and the development level seemed appropriate. *Kriegie 7956* would be geared for middle-school students. I seized the moment to "test-drive" my idea.

Last spring, we had the first draft of *Kriegie 7956* ready in time for our "Heroes' Welcome," and I read it to my students. Their response told me that we had something. I think they liked the humor, the drama, the suspense, and the fact that it was a history lesson with a human side. They learned about the geography of war as the stories of bombing mission locations and "the *Kriegie* march" unfolded. They learned about the unified effort of all Allied countries with examples of the overwhelming support of the war effort back home. They saw an art medium, the "Greene graphic," as an art form developed out of necessity and optimism. They relished the science moment (as did I), when they learned that membership in the Caterpillar Club is achieved only if one's life has been spared as the result of a silk parachute—made by silkworm caterpillars. As I continued the story, they laughed and they worried. Their hearts ached and soared—all in one book. I had them.

They began to tell me some of their stories that they had heard from their relatives. I encouraged them to talk to their relatives and put those stories down on paper. That result is one of the main reasons for writing the book. *Kriegie 7956* is *our* family record and tribute, but we hope it is also a vehicle for understanding and documenting veterans' experiences in any war fought for American freedoms.

The experience of writing the book has been a real learning experience for us. Dad likes to tell me that I'm the boss and the author. I like to tell Dad that he lived it and talked about it. I just wrote about it. I finally convinced him that both of our names should be listed as authors, and in October 1993, he wrote to me, saying, "If God was my 'copilot,' then you be my 'coauthor.' Could not ask for a better pair." So we have had a wonderful relationship through the evolution of *Kriegie 7956.* We thought that the work was over after the idea was down on paper. Two years ago this summer, the staff of Lot's Wife Publishing (Nancy Sorrells, Sue Simmons, and Katharine Brown) met with Dad and me to determine how we could get this story in print. One option was to do it locally with Lot's Wife Publishing, but we opted for Nancy's suggestion that we put together a proposal to White Mane Publishing Company, which has a youth division. That winter I worked on submission materials, and that spring we submitted the idea with sample chapters to White Mane. Things have been pretty fast-paced since then. The researching, rewriting, scanning, faxing, e-mailing, phoning, and documenting of this manuscript have taken on a life of their own. Dad has relished the work and I have become addicted to it. Through it all, we knew that we had something worthwhile, so we persevered. Over the past few months, when things got overwhelming, we ran to Nancy, who became our in-town editor and White Mane liaison. She calmed me down and offered suggestions for editing, layout, contractual concerns, and book sponsorship. Her resourcefulness, expertise, editorial savvy, and good humor have served us well. To her we owe our sincere gratitude and thanks.

The story would not even BE a story without the experience of Second Lieutenant Vernon L. Gatewood, or "Dad," my father-in-law of almost 29 years. His memory, his attention to detail in business matters, and his written documentation of the experience have provided us with quite an opportunity to share. Dad's ability to find humor in stressful situations has served him well over the years, and recently has enabled us not to take everything too seriously in this business of writing. That helped us to stay focused and gave us a needed laugh. Thank you for giving me the pleasure and honor of putting your experiences onto paper.

To Mark, my husband, goes my utmost thanks and love for supporting me in this project. As the project developed, he understood my mission to document his father's story using my middle-school perspective. He has always told me that I take on more than I should, but with this project we both knew that it was worthwhile. Without asking or prompting, he assumed household and family duties that would put other husbands to shame. Because of his willingness to "pick up the slack" at home since I was preoccupied with editing or researching, the book became a reality. He is my understanding, supportive, and loving soul mate and friend. Thank you, Mark, for all you are and all you do.

Betsy, my 16-year-old daughter, deserves my love and thanks for allowing me to use her name and ideas in the story. She was the inspiration for the perspective of the first chapter and final story line. She has been my number one student, and the one in whom I want to invest most of my energies—teaching, learning, loving. Mother/daughter disputes over computer time were sometimes awkward and the times I "stressed out" over malfunctioning computer programs were frustrating for us both. We came to understandings since we see that the project is bigger than any of our disagreements. She continues to inspire us, reward us, and make us proud with her new endeavors in high school. She is a love and a delight. Thank you, Honey, for understanding and helping.

I feel that I inherited my strong work ethic from my parents, Ernie and Betty Belkham. If they were here today, I know that they would be proud of our work in this family project that was inspired by the granddaughter they never knew. My brother, Ernie, who is a Vietnam veteran, encouraged me from the onset of the project, and helped me understand the loneliness and personal isolation of war. Maybe sometime we'll tell *his* war experiences. These strong family ties have helped me throughout this project in so many ways.

Researching for *Kriegie 7956* took many directions and required creative methods. My friend and media specialist at S. Gordon Stewart Middle School, Susan Thacker, tells my students when I have them in the library researching for my class, "That's why it is called 'RE-search.' You won't find all your answers in one place." How true those words played out for me. Not only did Susan give me that to reflect upon, but she gave help, advice, support, and encouragement in the project. Denise Brady, children's librarian and my former supervisor at Staunton Public Library, took time to confirm that there just weren't too many books about prisoners of war or World War II geared for middle-school students, and she encouraged me to change that. Steve Tabscott, circulation assistant at Staunton Public Library, assisted me often in finding just that specific resource that I couldn't find on my own. Ernest Thode and

Virginia Pritchett of Washington County Public Library in Marietta, Ohio, worked diligently to find documentation for the newspaper article entitled "How Next of Kin Get Word," referred to in *Kriegie 7956*. Jan Porter, Betsy's unofficial godmother, dear friend, and librarian at Richards Memorial Library in Paxton, Massachusetts, has encouraged me and assisted in research methods. To all the librarians I give special thanks for their hard work and persistence.

The Internet has made my research immediate in areas that otherwise would have taken weeks to do. I must give credit to some wonderful Web pages on military history and military procedures: Petty Girls nose art; The Collings Foundation, which has the only surviving (and still flying) B-24; the 450th Bombardment Group (the Cottontails); B-24s and heavybombers; Stalag Luft III-Sagan POW camp; Stalag VII A-Moosburg POW camp; the Cigarette Camps; and American Ex-Prisoners of War. Complete Web site addresses are listed in the bibliography.

Information about the "Greene graphic," the U.S. Code of Conduct, and POW camp maps was gained via e-mail, fax, and phone contacts. Many thanks to Roch Thornton of the *Kansas City Star* for helping us look for former Kansas City graphic artist Floyd H. Greene, Jr. Roch, an editor for the *Star* and Vietnam veteran in search of his Vietnam buddies, expressed support of my endeavor to document war experiences for generations to come. Steve Berge saw my inquiry in the POW archives and responded with scanned photos of other Greene graphics that he found in a thrift store in California. We utilized the public record information services, U.S. Search.com, Yahoo People Search, and the Social Security Death Index in our search for Floyd H. Greene, Jr., but after an exhaustive search we had no positive responses to any of our inquiries. In February 2000, we contracted with the U.S. Copyright Office to determine whether the copyright on the Greene graphic had been renewed. In their search, it was determined that the artwork had not been renewed within the 28th year of the first term of the copyright, and therefore copyright protection expired permanently at that time.

The U.S. Military Code of Conduct was posted by Rod Powers, on the usmilitary.about.com Guide U.S. Military Web site. Joseph Stomiany of La Miranda, California, corresponded with me about maps for German POW camps and shared his experiences as a *Kriegie* in Sagan, Nürnberg, and Moosburg POW camps. Thanks to William R. "Dick" Cubbins, of Natural Bridge, Virginia, and author of *The War of the Cottontails,* for assisting in the search for maps for our book. The American Ex-Prisoners of War POW Medsearch

Committee kindly granted permission for the one-time use of the German Prison Camps map in our book.

When Dad's friends in Marietta heard about the book, they expressed tremendous support and enthusiasm for the project. Bob Wagner, longtime friend and former business associate at Marietta Concrete, encouraged Dad and offered assistance in the search for newspaper article documentation at Washington County Public Library. His technical support and friendship have been invaluable in our project. Becky Madine, parish nurse of St. Luke's Lutheran Church in Marietta, continues to provide spiritual advice and grief counseling for Dad since Mom passed away in June 1998. After reading the first draft, she wrote that "...this book will enlighten those who are unfamiliar with this time in our history, and will be a nostalgic reminder for those who survived it." Many thanks for her guidance, encouragement, and continued assistance in the everyday challenge of surviving without Mom.

As a youngster, Dad's cousin Charles "Bud" Pickering followed Dad's war experiences in Marietta papers and considered Dad his hero. His comments after reading the first draft of the book were very flattering. He was impressed with the way the book was presented. "...A teacher's desire to keep history alive. A youth impressed by a story that could only be told by Grandpa. Wrapping the whole

WWII story into your granddaughter's education [by] passing the pursuit of freedom." Thank you for your perceptive and kind words.

Terry Silvester, of Shalimar, Florida, family friend and career military officer, gave support and testimonial to the work, and for that reason we asked him to write the foreword for *Kriegie 7956*. Thank you, Terry, for your military reflections and your on-target analysis of why stories like this need to be told.

My colleagues, educators Linda Petzke, Susan Thacker, Peggy Beck, and Sue Simmons, I thank for the inspiration and continued encouragement in this project. If I made any historical blunders or research documentation errors, I take complete blame. Thank you, Sue, for allowing me to use your classroom as a stage and your teaching technique as a vehicle for introducing the story. I am so glad that we worked together and that we continue to chart new territory for our projects. Special thanks go to Dr. Katharine Brown of Lot's Wife Publishing for opening the door to this new endeavor of writing. My computer guru and S. Gordon Stewart Middle School principal, Don D. Curtis, deserves the "Techno Award" for answering all my computer queries and for assisting in the scanning and transferring of files for presentations and publisher submission.

Five veterans' groups have donated funds for *Kriegie 7956*. Their commitment to the book has been encouraging and overwhelming. We certainly appreciate the kind donations from the Staunton, Virginia, Veterans of Foreign Wars Post #2216, Women's Auxiliary (Mary Kelley and Daisy Huff, treasurers); the Veterans of Foreign Wars Post #2216, Bingo Account (Earl Harris, Jr. and Don Hall); the Verona, Virginia, Veterans of Foreign Wars Post #10826 (Eugene Chavis); the Marietta, Ohio Veterans of Foreign Wars Post # 5108, Bingo Account (Judy McLeish and Ronnie Davis, treasurers); and the American Ex-Prisoners of War, Mid-Ohio Valley Chapter #15 (Gifford B. Doxsee, treasurer). We thank you for your support and votes of confidence.

The staff at White Mane has been especially patient and helpful to these novice writers. Harold Collier has always responded succinctly and promptly to my many questions. Alexis Handerahan has been extremely helpful, friendly, and upbeat in the last frantic weeks before the submission deadline. Her encouraging words made me feel that *Kriegie 7956* WOULD be a reality within a few months.

This experience of putting Dad's words into my format has been challenging, fulfilling, inspiring, and educational. I hope that I have done justice to his story. Dad and

I sincerely hope that *Kriegie 7956* will encourage the youth of today to take a closer look at family and world history, and to vow to continue the pursuit of freedom for all generations of Americans to come.

Betty Jean Belkham Gatewood
March 24, 2001
Mt. Sidney, Virginia

INTRODUCTION

World War II, or "The Good War," had the total commitment of all Americans to the war effort. On the battlefields, in enemy airspace, in prison camps, and at home, our democratic freedoms were pursued by so many heroes. That is a new concept for some middle-school students, since perhaps the most recent war stories that they might have heard were of Vietnam, when antiwar demonstrations got as much press coverage as the battles, or of the Gulf War in which reasons for the war were fuzzy and laced with economic overtones.

Children need to understand the sacrifices and cherish the freedoms that have been fought for them. All children need to take ownership of their family history, and this story enabled my daughter to see how our family history helped shape American history. Some freedom fighters paid the highest price for us—the ultimate sacrifice of their lives. As my father-in-law frequently mentioned as we worked on this project, World War II veterans are dying at the rate of one thousand per day. Stories have been, and are being lost and buried, but this story lives on. *Kriegie*

7956 was just too important a story *not* to be told. Family history and American history became intertwined in this true story of love, humor, bravery, heroism, survival, and perseverance in the face of adversity. Let's hope that this one is the beginning of many stories saved.

"...simple faith in the freedom of democracy" is worth fight-ing for.

—Speech by Franklin D. Roosevelt
Staunton, Virginia, May 4, 1941

CHAPTER 1

THE ASSIGNMENT

Betsy's eyes widened in surprise at the grade on her world history paper—only a "B." She wasn't ashamed of it, but she was disappointed. She really thought that her essay about the Great Depression would have earned her an "A." She had done her research in encyclopedias and on the Internet, she had listened intently in class, she had read her text and used correct grammar, but on the last page of her paper, Mrs. Simmons had written, *"Nice job—good general information. An improvement would have been to find personal accounts in primary sources. That's where you'd find the emotions, feelings and reactions to events of the time. An essay gives feeling and opinion. Form your own opinions by letting people help you understand the history—they were there...."* Betsy was reading her paper and the comments over and over again, but was brought back to the present when Mrs. Simmons mentioned the next theme and new assignment. She was talking about a prophetic speech given in Staunton by President Franklin Roosevelt at the dedication of the Woodrow Wilson Birthplace in 1941. Roosevelt's theme had been fighting for freedoms and democracy, and he was right here in her hometown when he said those words. That made it more real. Betsy was beginning to understand what Mrs. Simmons meant. Now she had moved on to World War II, and class discussion focused on events leading up to the war, the overwhelming support of, and dedication to the war effort by all Americans.

"You would be surprised to learn about some of the adventures of people that shaped the history of the world during this time. In our country, Americans were amazingly united in their desire to win the war; it was a 'popular war.' Basic freedoms were being threatened in the world, so Americans knew that the war must be won to preserve those freedoms. Everyone was involved with the war effort in one way or another. Your assignment is to find someone who lived during World War II—maybe an adult who remembers collecting scrap metal when he was a child, maybe a young wife who stayed home working and worrying while her husband was off at war, or maybe a veteran, if you can find one. Sadly, this wonderful population of freedom fighters is dying at the rate of one thousand per day. Find them. Interview him or her, ask for experiences, hardships, sacrifices and their duty. Your goal is to learn from them. Find out how they felt about their duties, why they did what they did, and how they were involved in our country's fight for freedom. Don't be surprised if they are reluctant to talk because some memories might still be painful. I can pretty much assure you, however, that once they feel comfortable talking, they will fill you with stories of honor, duty to country and personal sacrifice. Most will downplay their roles; humility is a strong suit with that generation. So, be gentle in your questioning and maybe you'll be rewarded by letting *them* teach you the history by their experiences. That is the perfect primary source."

That assignment was the major project for this part of the semester and due in three weeks. How was she going to find time to do it? She was finding that high school was more demanding than middle school. More assignments, more homework, more big projects. She had been looking forward to a soon-to-come rest from all the school work. Spring vacation was the following week, but now, since this assignment, she knew she'd be thinking and worrying about it. Her family was planning on traveling to Ohio to visit her grandparents during the vacation. Then she had the idea— maybe this was the time to ask Grandpa some questions about the war, since he was a veteran. Betsy remembered he had been in World War II and his plane was shot down. He parachuted down, but was captured by the Germans and spent about nine months in several German prisoner of war camps. On a few occasions over the years, she had heard her grandparents reminiscing about "The Good War," but she never heard or understood many details. She remembered hearing a little about how their wedding celebration was cut short by a new set of military orders. She remembered a few references to Grandpa being a POW, and that for some reason he did not like Jell-O or cold weather because of his experiences. That was about all she knew—it was a mysterious part of her family's history. There must be a bigger story there, and she wondered why they didn't talk about it. Maybe it *was* too painful. Betsy wondered if now, since she had a serious reason and sincere desire to know about it, maybe she could coax some stories from them—if they were willing. Her worrying about *when* to get the assignment done was beginning to turn to worrying about *how* to get her grandparents to share their wartime experiences with her.

Two days later, Betsy and her family were on their way to Ohio to visit her grandparents for Easter. Even though Betsy had several hours of travel time to figure out how she was going to begin "her research," she was still undecided about how to get started. The solution presented itself as the family pulled into her grandparents' driveway.

Grandpa's car license plate read "Former POW...." Betsy had seen it so many times, but now it had new meaning to her.

Later that afternoon, after they exchanged the gifts that they had stored away for one another, Betsy asked Grandpa about his POW license plate and the photo she noticed on the wall above the breakfast bar. This area is admittedly a unique collage of family snapshots, framed photos, paintings, cross-stitches, granddaughter gifts, and other memorabilia. These items are treasured mementos of events, vacations, and holidays that have special meaning to all of them. A photo of special interest to her was one of Grandpa and another man shaking hands across the POW license plate on the rear of his car.

"That's Captain Kelly when we visited him in South Carolina last winter. He was the pilot and I was the bombardier of a B-24 during World War II," her grandpa explained.

That's a beginning, thought Betsy. She plunged ahead, "What did you do as a bombardier? Where were you stationed? Where were you when you parachuted out of your plane? What was it like in prisoner of war camp? Were you able to write letters to Grandma from prison? Did you get any medals? When did your——"

Grandpa was overwhelmed and nervously began to laugh. After a pause to collect his thoughts, he said, "For so many years I tried to forget all of those things. It was not a happy time; I don't know if I can remember....I do have some note cards with 'buzz words' that reminded me about certain things that happened in the war. Your grandmother kept a scrapbook of that time, and she kept a lot of papers too—telegrams, newspaper clippings, photos in a little wooden box. At one time we were going to write a book. I started it, but work and fatherhood came first. Sometime maybe we'll see about all that. For right now, let's get ready to go out to dinner. You all must be starved after your long drive!"

At dinner and during the next few days of their visit, Betsy tried to get her grandpa to tell her about his experiences, but she couldn't get more than just a few sentences from him. She felt frustrated about getting her assignment done, but more than that, she felt sad about not knowing this part of her family's history. Maybe her timing wasn't right, or maybe those thoughts *were* too painful to remember.

Back at home a few days later, Betsy received a small package from Grandpa. She excitedly opened the package—it wasn't Christmas, and not even close to her birthday. She wondered what it was. Inside were two audio tapes, some papers in a little wooden box, and a note that read:

> Dear Betsy, I have attempted to answer some
> of your questions about my war experiences on

these tapes. It was somewhat difficult to do, but strangely enough, I found it easy to talk into the tape recorder. Yesterday, Grandma and I decided to get out my 'buzz cards,' the scrapbook, and this little keepsake box where she kept those papers I mentioned. I hope this helps you understand about 'The Big War,'—or 'The Good War'—as we sometimes call it. I have done this because I feel that you and young people your age must know about the war—why we did it and how we did it. All of what you hear is true.

World War II was fought to protect our freedoms. Freedom is precious—learn to love it and respect it. Sometimes freedom does not come cheap or easy, but it is always a worthwhile pursuit. Love, Grandpa.

With anticipation and respect for the effort that must have gone into preparing the package, Betsy loaded the first tape into her tape player, opened the little wooden box, pressed "play," and sat back for her history lesson.

Chapters two through nine tell the experiences of Lieutenant Vernon L. "Gate" Gatewood....

The Following-named 2d Lt, AC, Class No. 44-5, having completed the required course of instruction at the AAFBS, Big Spring AA Fld, Big Spring, Tex, is rated Aircraft Observer (Bombardier), effective 8 Apr 44: Gatewood, Vernon L. #0717885

—Personnel Orders, Headquarters Army Air Forces Central
Flying Training Command

Randolph Field, Texas, 10 March 1944

CHAPTER 2
DUTY CALLS

Let me begin by stating that war is a deadly serious business, with accent on the "deadly." I can attest to this fact having expended some nine months of my life and some fifty pounds of my limb in various prisons, camps, and prison camps from Vienna, Austria to Moosburg, Germany in World War II. I was just one of the thousands who directed their energies toward the goal of securing freedom and democracy in the world. It was a time of tremendous patriotism and support of our president, our government, and its policies. In spite of my difficulties during the war, I maintained the faith that our government was doing the right thing in fighting the war to secure free-doms for all. There was never any question as to why we were in the war; everyone knew we were doing the right thing by doing what we were trained to do. It was an intense and frightening time for me, but it was not without humorous moments. Sometimes finding the humor was difficult, but I'm convinced that humor made some of the circumstances bearable. So here is "my story."

In 1942 I was working for our family friend, Leonard Christy, as a clerk at Marietta Concrete Corporation in the Scotia, New York, plant. Marietta Concrete made all kinds of silos and in this plant our main product was farm silos. I had a deferment, which meant that I was excused from being drafted to go into the service because I was in an industry that was critical to the war effort—agriculture. But my problem was that the deferment was a short one and since it was given to me by the draft board, I would be drafted eventually because my deferment would expire soon. If I was drafted, I would not have any choice as to what branch of service or what type of position in the military I would be. I wanted to fly, and I had always wanted to be a bombardier. I was tired of being deferred and I wanted to be able to choose my branch and type of service. So on September 27, 1942, I enlisted in the army air force at the Aviation Cadet Examining Board in Albany, New York. I then went home to Marietta and prepared to enter my chosen service.

I was an eager, excited, yet apprehensive 23 year old when I left Marietta that fall. I traveled by train to the induction center in Fort Thomas, Kentucky, where I was to be trained and assigned. One of my earliest memories of this new adventure was that meals were no longer served on plates but were scooped from one large metal pail by a small metal pail onto another metal pail called a mess kit and eaten with a large metal spoon! Another memory deals with my acquiring the role of Uncle Sam's Number One *snafu* boy—with very little effort on my part!—*Snafu* was military slang for <u>s</u>ituation <u>n</u>ormal, <u>a</u>ll <u>f</u>ouled <u>up</u>.—We used this term to describe some of the silly, inexplainable, frustrating things that happened to us. It seemed that I was the object of lots of mix-ups—*snafus*. I guess I should have known from the first day that things would be different.

On our first day, all four hundred of us were gathered together on a basketball court covered with double decker bunks. I relaxed on a top bunk.—I wanted a lower bunk, but I lost a coin toss for it.—We were to find out which of us would go where, as our names were called out in alphabetical order. A big burly sergeant bawled out our names, but he didn't say my name at the "Gs." I began to get a little uneasy when he got around to the "Ms," but felt that since my name started with "G," they might have me listed as *Mr.* Gatewood under the "Ms." By the time he ran through the "Vs"—for *Vernon*—, I began to realize that they did not even have me listed under first names.

Now I was really concerned, because I have always believed in safety in numbers. Also this was the only time I could ever have considered myself one of the four hundred, and I did not want to relinquish this position. By this time the sergeant had completed his roll call and I was not even among the ones he could not pronounce. For the first time in my military career, I volunteered,—"Would the sergeant please check his list for my name once more?" He glared down at me and said that if he had not called out my name, then it just was not on the list. I think that they had lost my records. I had visions of going back home with my one day's service, but he said if my name were not called, then I would wait here until someone DID call it. Did you ever sleep alone on a basketball court covered with two hundred double decker bunks? I didn't sleep much that first night because of all those lower bunks to choose from! I think that was the first and last time I had a choice of much of anything.

Two days later, my name turned up from someplace and I found myself on a troop train headed for Keesler Field, Mississippi. These troop trains were converted milk trains with the same stops,—but no one got off—and same refrigeration! Three days and one head cold later, we debarked at Keesler Field. There we were informed that there was a war on and that there was a shortage of uniforms, and we were asked to kindly wear the clothes we had until a new shipment of clothing came in. It was here that I decided to reread the instructions that had been enclosed in our orders. Sure enough they said not to bring more than one change of clothing, since we would soon be in the uniform of the USA. For five days the uniform of the day was one mussed sport jacket and one white shirt that I wore for everything—marching, meals, and calisthenics. At last we were issued clothing, and thankfully, most of mine fit.

It was at Keesler Field that I learned about obstacle courses. Obstacle courses are designed to build up the body and the resistance. My body stayed the same, but my resistance was certainly built up—to obstacle courses that is.

Some days later, we were on our way to Tuscaloosa, Alabama, for pre-aviation training at the University of Alabama for CTD—College Training Detachment. I spent time in the hospital there because the head cold that I developed on that milk train had developed into a "full blown" case of bronchitis, complete with a ruptured septum in my nose. But I healed, I had uniforms, and I decided I had a pretty good thing in Tuscaloosa. Now was the time to invite my fiancée down for a wedding—*ours*. She was to arrive by train, but because I couldn't leave the base, I couldn't meet her. We planned our wedding from her hotel room via the phone. We got married the afternoon of May 13, 1943. I got half a day off to attend the ceremony, but I was told I could not have the night out. Much later that night, as I crawled back up the fire escape to my room, I was given the news that I was one of the lucky 50 men chosen to be shipped out next morning at 6:00 to San Antonio, Texas. There I was to be given all the tests for pre-flight aviation cadet training. I would rather have spent some more time and passed a couple more courses at Tuscaloosa, but I did not press the point. Another *snafu* happened that next morning when we almost missed our train because our train commander took us to the wrong train station! When our mistake was discovered, we were loaded on a truck and rushed to the correct station. Luckily the train was a half hour late, so we did make it, but not without leaving quite a chuckle for those still in Tuscaloosa. I did not see your grandma for four months after our first short evening together.

After exhaustive tests at San Antonio, I was informed that I had qualified for bombardier training and would be sent to Houston, Texas, for pre-flight schooling. I have now forgotten just about all the facts and figures I stuffed into my eager little brain during those months of training. Generally, I learned how to do my job as a bombardier on an aircraft called a B-24. I learned to sight in and decide when to drop the bombs. Just let's say that I graduated into the role of "an officer and a gentleman" with wings on my blouse, bars on my shoulder, and a desire to become a stateside flight instructor in my heart, but I really *was* ready to go overseas to help if needed. I put all my efforts toward the war and acting against "the enemy." I graduated and received my commission on April 8, 1944, in Big Spring, Texas, and my new wife joined me there for the ceremony. Shortly after my graduation, I had "leave" or vacation and I went home to Marietta.

During a leisurely dinner there with my folks and my wife, I got a telegram that I had to report to Westover Field, Massachusetts, where I would be assigned to a combat crew. My wife and I were soon on our way to Massachusetts. Of course, Grandma was not to be assigned, she just wanted to be with me as long as possible because I was being prepared for going overseas. I was given LOTS of immunizations to prepare for going to a foreign country. I remember that your grandma had to pay for dinner that night—my arm was so sore that I couldn't reach my wallet in my back pocket for me to pay!

Lieutenant and Mrs. Vernon L. Gatewood, April 1944, Marietta, Ohio

Finally the big day I had been waiting for arrived—the assignment of B-24 crews. I will always carry with me the memory of the first meeting of our crew. My pilot—Captain Kelly, whom you saw in the POW photo on our memory wall—turned to the copilot and said, "You mean we have to take *him*?" This friendly bantering went on until the commanding officer verified that I was part of the crew. Crew #218 was made up of four officers: Captain Earle Kelly—pilot, Second Lieutenant Robert Rinschler—copilot, First Lieutenant Lessing Kahn—navigator, me—Second Lieutenant—bombardier. The 10-member crew was complemented with six enlisted men: Sergeant Richard Gordon, Corporal Willis Paschal, Sergeant Caspar Mione, Corporal Charles Becker, Sergeant Burl Barker, and Corporal Buford Evans. These airmen handled the other guns and various duties on board.

My official job as bombardier was to sight in and drop bombs on assigned targets. My unofficial duties were to keep out of the way on all flights and on long flights to see that all crew members were well supplied with fruit juices and Cokes. We cooled the drinks by placing them in the glassed-in machine gun turrets in the front of the plane where I sat. One of my jobs was supposed to have been to man the top gun turret, but after a few near misses, my crew decided to confine my talents to bombs only. As they gently put it, "After all, a bomb can go only one way—

down." I guess they all felt safer with me handling the bombs instead of the turret machine guns!

During training, I learned how to maneuver in my cramped quarters and to keep from being stepped on by the navigator. My position in the nose of the B-24 was directly under the navigator, who was directly under the pilot and copilot. I had to squeeze into this tiny space first—it was very cramped—and often I did get stepped on. After several short weeks of being checked out in our new B-24, we were notified that the day had come and we were to prepare to fly overseas. We were assigned to the Charleston, South Carolina, base for final preparations. Your grandma joined me there and we had a little house that we rented for a couple of months with another service couple. We enjoyed our time together in South Carolina, then in July we were assigned to Mitchell Field, New York, from where I was to depart.

Your grandma was so supportive through all this military moving around. When I was stationed where she couldn't be with me, she stayed in Marietta and worked. When my orders allowed, she traveled to where I was, so she could be with me. She joined me in Tuscaloosa while I was in pre-aviation training—that's when we got married. She was with me in Texas for graduation, Massachusetts for crew training, South Carolina for final preparations, then on to Mitchell Field, New York, for shipping out. When I was overseas in Italy and later as a POW in Germany, she kept the scrapbook, wrote letters, and sent packages to me. I always knew that she was waiting for me. She was great. She was among those millions who also served by waiting.

You might wonder about "the enemy." At this time, free people of the world knew that democracy and freedoms were being threatened by dictators in Europe. Our country was founded on basic freedoms that we decide on or vote on together. Our method of government, called democracy, is where the citizens vote to make laws about those freedoms. Some countries in the world have or had governments where *one* person decides what is best for all citizens in the country. This type of government, called a dictatorship, was the case in Germany in the 1930s and 1940s. People there were not allowed to have their own political views, and were often threatened, terrorized, and in many cases, eliminated because of their heritage, their politics, or their beliefs.

In Germany, Adolf Hitler ran the country by his own personal rules. He had done some progressive things to help Germans out of an economic depression in the 1930s, so his countrymen revered him. But they also feared him. He and his followers, the Nazis, disregarded freedom, democracy, and human decency. Adolf Hitler was power hungry—he wanted to dominate as many people and countries as he could. For one thing, he felt there should be only one race of people whom he called the "Aryan" race. He tried to create his perfect race through *ethnic cleansing*—killing people of races different than the one he believed to be his superior race. Millions of Jews and other "undesirables" were enslaved or killed to satisfy his wishes. He began to take over smaller, weaker countries in Europe by enslaving their peoples to improve the desperate, war conditions for Germans. Hitler tried to convince other European countries that his plan for the world was good. The best way to describe him is to say he was a malevolent zealot—an egotistical, spiteful, nasty, twisted fanatic. He had to be stopped so democracy could survive.

Many countries that enjoyed freedom and democracy—like the United States, Britain, and France—realized that Hitler was dangerous, and one by one, they declared war on him and his country. There was no one in America who thought that going to war was a bad idea. There was national pride and support for the war effort. The battle lines were easily drawn up. President Roosevelt led us with wisdom and charisma and we eagerly followed his lead. Unlike the recent Vietnam War, in which your Uncle Ernie served in the 1960s, World War II was a popular war. All Americans did what they could for the war effort. Everyone in the free world was in agreement that Hitler should be stopped. He was the enemy that we fought against. I don't know where I first heard this quote, but it

rings so true: "We all gave some, and many gave ALL"—
the supreme gift for freedom: their lives. We must remember that and be forever thankful for their sacrifices.

We could recognize the anti-aircraft or flak fire by the dreaded, nasty, little black bursts of smoke.

—Lieutenant Vernon Gatewood

Chapter 3
Flak!

After several short weeks of being checked out in our new B-24, we were notified that the day had come and we were to prepare to fly overseas. By now, I was beginning to suspect that any hopes of becoming a flight instructor in "The States" were practically nil, but I was still willing. I was also willing to do what my officers told me to do.

My overseas preparations consisted of filling one foot-locker with Hershey bars and long underwear. I had heard that chocolate bars were great for barter with the Italians, but to this day cannot figure why I had all those pairs of long underwear. This shouldn't have bothered me though, because as you may have guessed, I never saw either again. Leaving your grandmother was really hard, but we both knew that it was a duty and honor to serve our country. That didn't make the actual departure any easier, however—

it was a tearful goodbye. It was then that she gave me this picture of her that I carried throughout the war, even in POW camp. It kept me going through all my hardships (see next page).

My crew left Mitchell Field, New York, on July 21, 1944, and after several stops and quite a few delays, we arrived in Manduria, Italy, on August 14. From there we would take off into the "wild, blue yonder" with real bullets and bombs. After having trained for many hours in the air, the "wild blue" did not bother me, but I did wonder about the "yonder." I found out that they didn't need flight instructors there either, so I gave up all hopes of teaching and decided to put all my efforts toward acting against the enemy. This was my duty now—to fly missions on my B-24.

Officially, I was now a member of the 15th Army Air Corps-450th Bomber Group, 722 Squadron, Crew #218. Our bomber group was nicknamed the "Cottontails" because of the white vertical rudders on the big tail of our B-24s. Our bomber, a four-engine B-24 Liberator, was the workhorse bomber of the war. It could fly farther, faster at higher altitudes, AND with more bombs than the more famous B-17, or Flying Fortress. "Bare Dog" was the radio name of our plane and there was a Petty Girl painted on it as nose art. Most of the planes were adorned with artwork on the nose, and George Petty was a famous artist whose work found its way onto many aircraft in World War II. I

Picture of Mrs. Norma Jean Gatewood, May 1944, that was carried by Lieutenant Gatewood throughout his military service overseas

don't remember the name of the plane, but I do remember that beautiful, leggy girl which was characteristic of "Petty Girls." Most of our flying and dropping of bombs was at an altitude of about 20–22,000 feet. Our plane was well protected with machine guns in the nose, tail, top, and bottom turrets and sides.

The uniform that we were issued was summer weight cotton, but when we flew at those high altitudes, we had shearling, or wool fleece-lined, leather flight jackets and pants that we wore over our summer suits. We wore "Lindbergh-like" helmets, oxygen masks, and "throat mikes" so we could communicate with one another, and leather boots. On missions we were also issued *flak* suits. A flak suit consisted of a metal helmet and a jacket that was somewhat like the padded, protective vests that police officers wear today. They were bulky, hard to maneuver in, but created at least in our minds some mental protection from *flak*. *Flak* is a shortened term or slang for the German word *Fliegerabwehrkanone* or anti-aircraft guns. The Germans had their important and strategic positions surrounded by flak and we were pretty much defenseless against it, despite our machine guns. The flak shells could travel from the ground positions up to us at 20,000+ feet. At that altitude, they burst into lots of fragments that could not only damage us, but the plane itself. These fragments could ignite the fuel and destroy the plane. Not to get too technical, but the B-24s had what was called a "Davis wing" that was exceptionally narrow. If we were hit and disabled, the chances of our plane coasting back to our base were slimmer because we had less surface for gliding. We pretty much expected the anti-aircraft or flak fire, and we could recognize it by the dreaded, nasty, little black bursts of smoke.

As an item of survival, we were issued fine silk neck scarves, which were actually maps of the theater of war in which we were operating. It was thought that if we were shot down in unfamiliar territory, this would help us find our way back to a friendly area. We wore two pairs of gloves: a heavy, wool-lined leather pair and a lightweight silk pair. When I was fine-tuning the bombsight on a mission, I would only wear the silk pair by themselves for the delicate touch needed. It was cold up there at 22,000 feet! Our navigator, Lessing Kahn, really did not like the cold, so he located something called an electric suit. It was somewhat like a long underwear outfit, but it had wires in it for heat! He was hooked up to the electrical system in the plane, and I guess it worked fine, but on one mission, our electrical system was shot out. His return trip home was a cold one because he was only wearing the non-functioning electric suit and his underwear!

My main bombardier duty was to line up the target with the bombsight so we could drop the bombs. The new, top-secret Norden bombsight equipment that I used cal-culated the trajectory or pathway of the bombs according to what information I told it for wind direction and speed of the plane. While Captain Kelly, our pilot, put the plane on autopilot, I actually controlled the plane and pinpointed the target for the drop. The interaction between the bomb-sight, the information I gave it, and my sighting in of the target determined when the bombs would be dropped. It was work that necessitated concentration, and that was difficult because of the noisy, cold, cramped quarters, and distractions going on outside the plane, but we were pretty accurate. We had practiced over and over again with this new equipment on the ground in simulation towers and in training planes back in the States.

Besides being the bombardier and the cooler of Cokes, one of my duties back on base was to be mail censor for our crew. That meant that I had to read everyone's personal mail. I had to see whether there was any sensitive informa-tion that could get into the wrong hands if it was intercepted. We were entrusted with sensitive information relating to our mission and equipment, especially since we used the new bombsight equipment. During our flight training, we had to take the oath of the "bombardier's code" not to dis-close any information regarding the method with which we located targets or how we sighted them in. Censoring mail was a duty I dreaded—I felt it was an invasion of their privacy, but one that I understood was needed to insure the success of our mission.

I was quite a warrior, I thought—complete with tools needed for self-preservation. On my left hip, I carried an 11-inch hunting knife to cut my parachute cords if I became entangled with trees in bailing out—my stepfather had given it to me for just that purpose—, and on my right hip, I slung an Army .45 caliber automatic pistol in the event I became entangled with *enemy* people. Another reason why we were issued the .45 was so that we could keep the technology of the Norden bombsight equipment from getting into enemy hands. In the event that we were downed with the plane and bombsight intact, we were ordered to use the .45 to destroy the workings of the bombsight by putting a bullet right through the eyepiece. I had become so proficient with my cal .45 pistol that by now, I could dismantle and replace all the parts in two minutes—blindfolded. However, when it came to firing the weapon, the only way I could have hit the side of the proverbial barn was to have been inside with all the doors closed. Nevertheless, I took tender care of the pistol for I had plans for it. All these things, along with my government uniform parts, my A-2 leather flight jacket, a whopping pair of binoculars, a wrist watch, and an excellent quality briefcase, were to be my souvenirs of this thing called war. As it turned out, all the items became souvenirs, all right, but not mine.

I have several memories of being at our base in Manduria, Italy, even though I was there for only 10 complete missions—from August 14 to September 10, 1944. One of the most moving experiences was watching a disabled plane fly over the airfield. It was out of control and could not land. The pilot had evidently put it on autopilot and the 10 crew parachuted down to safety from the plane as it flew over. High on my list of things I'll never forget at Manduria was our first scheduled combat mission—the oil field of Ploesti, Romania. We had all heard about this target; it had been a frequent target for Allied missions. If we could take out the refinery, then this would severely cripple the fuel source and therefore the firepower of the German army. The targets were so well guarded with flak that it was lovingly named Purple Heart Alley. Of the 177 B-24s that were on the famous raid in August 1943 about one-third of the planes did not return. When this target was named at briefing, my hands were trembling so violently that I was unable to write out my resignation. I wasn't really serious about that resignation, but we were all worried about the mission. After the briefing session, we climbed into our cozy little aluminum cockpit and sat in the warm morning sun awaiting orders to take off and "give 'em hell, boys!" We were hot because we had all our flight gear on, and we were scared—that was a normal, accepted reaction when going into combat. We waited and whiled away the time with good-natured jokes about the brass at General Headquarters, how warm it was getting, and how could one be so warm with heat and cold with fear at the same time?

Finally, after two hours of waiting, we were told that due to weather over the target, the strike had been called off for the day. We were so disappointed by this news that we jumped the six feet to the ground instead of getting out the conventional way.

In some of my early missions I became well acquainted with flak and the various means of protecting against it. I was the only bombardier in the outfit who could pull a flak helmet down over my head all the way to my knees and yell "bombs away" at the same time. My hobby at that time was a form of posture control known as "how's this for a small target?" To my dismay one day, I discovered that these deadly little fragments could come from any direction. On one particular bomb run, I recall, I was making some delicate last minute adjustments to the bombsight on the bomb run, when I heard a dull *whump*, followed by a rush of air. Without raising my head, I glanced sideways and saw a small hole in the side of the nose of the plane about the size of a golf ball. Turning the other direction, I found the exit of the missile had left a hole the size of a golf BAG. This was about six inches from where

I was crouching at my bombsight. From that time on, I always approved of the golf rule that caused the Good Lord to call "fore!" in time for me to duck out of the line of flight, AND I was always first in line when flak suits and helmets were being issued.

This type of thing went on for some weeks during which time I picked up 10 complete combat missions, and was mentally counting the days until I could complete enough "'round trippers" to enable me to go to Rome, Italy, for a short rest. This was, according to those fortunate few who had finally made the necessary 25 missions, "a heaven on earth." At this point I still had faith that I would get possession of my Hershey bars in time for that little jaunt to Rome.

When questioned, should I become a prisoner of war, I am required to give name, rank, service number, and date of birth. I will evade answering further questions to the utmost of my ability.

—U.S. Military Code of Conduct, Article 5

CHAPTER 4
BAILOUT AT 20,000 FEET

I never made it to Rome with my Hershey bars, because my next mission was my last. Early on September 10, 1944, we lumbered into the air on a mission to destroy a tank factory in Vienna, Austria. After 10 complete missions, at last I was about to find out where the "yonder" really was in "the wild, blue yonder." The second thing I found out was that there wasn't nearly as much humor there as there had been prior to that day.

The day dawned clear as we rolled out for our 11th mission. Our target that day was a plant in Vienna that produced ball bearings for German tanks. We flew the flight to the initial point from where we would make final approach to the target, and as we approached, we could see black puffs of flak searching for our altitude. Through this we made our bomb run, dropped our bombs, and were just turning away from the target when we received flak hits in our number three and number four engines—both on the right side of the plane. This was very bad news, because with both engines out on the same side of the ship, control became extremely difficult, if not almost impossible. Also to add to our woes, the flak had damaged quite a few hydraulic lines running through the plane lengthwise, and fluids of all kinds were spraying through the bomb bay, an area where we had to go if we were going to get out. I took one look at our pilot, Captain Kelly, who was emphatically pointing down and yelling "GO!" at the same time. This meant we had to jump through the bomb bay doors. My first chore was to release the nose gunner from his turret, which I did, then I took off my flak suit and hooked on the chest parachute. I took off my leather gloves, leaving the silk-lined gloves on so I would be able to feel the rip cord when that time came. So, with no time to think about it, we jumped into 22,000 feet of nothing but cold, thin air.

I was impressed with the silence. The silence was so intense that it was deafening. I looked back and saw our plane blow up in the air. I saw a few chutes as I floated down, and I found out later that all 10 of the crew did parachute out. Although this was my first actual jump, we had been trained as to several "dos and don'ts" we should try to remember in such a situation. Fortunately some of these did come to my mind on my free fall.

#1: *Free fall until about 10,000 feet, then pull the rip cord.* When bailing out at 22,000 feet the air is so thin, you are apt to pass out from lack of oxygen. Training films had shown us that at 10,000 feet, large ground details like buses and trucks could be seen, and color could be detected. When we saw those things, we could pull the rip cord to open the chute. While doing my free fall for several thousand feet, I found that I really had a lot of control over my body. Going through the air was almost pleasant, and I even did some somersaults—although I should have been thinking about what lay ahead.

#2: *Be looking at nothing but sky when pulling the rip cord.* In the opening of the parachute, the shrouds or cords could tear at your face and damage it. In case we couldn't remember that, we were also told to leave our oxygen mask on until after we pulled the rip cord. If we had a problem with the shrouds, it would just mostly tear the mask from our face and not damage us too much. So, when I *thought* I was around 10,000 feet, I waited for the sky to show up, then I pulled the rip cord. I will never forget the shock of the chute actually opening. After having fallen that far and that fast, the opening of the chute was like a very, very sudden stop. In fact, I had the impression that I was going back up instead of down.

With the chute open now, I was coming down at a slower rate of speed. I thought, "Now it is time to take off the oxygen mask." This is how I got my first indication of how high and how alone I was. I held out the oxygen mask and just dropped it. I watched it go down, down, down...until it just finally dwindled out of my sight. To prove that your mind plays tricks on you even in the time of danger, all of a sudden, I thought, "I'm going to miss the USO show tonight!" It is funny that I was thinking of that during my predicament. Missing the show was the least of my worries, because by now I could see the ground coming up to meet me and I tried to remember something else.

#3: *Flex your knees when you hit the ground.* I remembered, but I hit the ground and injured my left ankle upon impact. I didn't even realize it because I was too busy trying to gather up my chute so I could hide it. I came down in a cornfield where there was a little wooded area near me. I tried to gather my chute and head for that wooded area thinking I could hide out there. However, my white parachute was quite a target as I was coming down. Little Hungarian soldiers with great big guns and silk hats had me covered all the way down. They encircled me and gave me indications that I should raise my hands—both hands—which I did.

At this point I should mention that although our target for bombing was in Vienna, Austria, I actually landed near a little town called Gyor in Hungary. When we got hit, we had just turned away from the target, and then during my bailout, I had drifted far away from the target. As to my captors, I must say that although we did not speak the same language, it is amazing how gestures with loaded guns get the intended message across. I never did find out exactly how the well-uniformed businesslike soldiers with fancy silk hats fitted into the German war picture, but Hungary was occupied by Hitler at that time. Although they were extremely businesslike in their actions, they were not brutal. Upon capture, I was taken to a small military encampment, possibly a police station, where I was held and questioned. I think that I was as much a curiosity item to them as they were to me. Various people were brought in who could speak English in order to aid in their questioning. I recall one very nice looking lady who said that she was a Hungarian countess, and if the situation were different she might have been able to help me. But she said that would endanger her own life. To show my gratitude, I gave her my last few American cigarettes which she seemed to value very highly. So much for any dramatic, romantic movielike try for escape. This was just not my best day.

I remembered some of the training films I had seen where we had been told that even though they were the enemy, some of our enemy outfits did respect military rank. At every opportunity, I pointed to the gold bar on my collar and said, "I'm an officer and expect to be treated as such." The only thing this got me was that they did appoint a low-ranking soldier to carry my chute and other items of my uniform while they put me in a two-wheeled cart. This they drove around showing off their trophy—*ME.* This cart took me to a small camp where I was put into solitary confinement. My .45 automatic pistol, my hunting knife, silk map scarf, and my parachute became the confiscated property of the bad guys for their future use. I wore only my summer weight uniform.

During my short stay at this Hungarian camp or garrison, I gained some insight as to how these people viewed and perceived the American people as a whole. This was done because one of the guards spoke a "certain kind" of English. I noticed that throughout our conversations there was a certain quality which sounded strangely like a Victrola record being played. A Victrola was an early brand of a record and record player, but the quality of the sound was inferior to today's recordings and players. When I quizzed him about his English, he admitted that was exactly how he had learned to speak English—by listening to American records being played. Chalk one up for me.

They certainly had a distorted view of America and Americans. First of all, they had been told that each

American airman was to receive $10,000 for each com-
pleted bombing mission! Not true, of course. Next they
had the impression that Chicago, Illinois, was a city completely overrun with corruption, crime, alcohol, and prosti-
tution. Chicago must have been run by Al Capone; his
henchmen and their activities were completely overlooked
by law enforcement. There was a grain of truth there, however. I defended Chicago, but not Al Capone! They DID
have access to some movies, and their nationwide hero
was Tom Mix, a leading Western movie star of the time. I
gave them that one—they were on target there. All of this
conversation still did not keep me out of solitary, however.
Solitary confinement accommodations consisted of boards
only for a bed with no mattress.

I was kept in the camp until they put me on a small
train that took me to Budapest. There I was once again
put into solitary confinement in a civil prison. I complained
that military prisoners were not to be put into civil prisons,
but that got me nothing but jeers.

During our training for combat, we had been briefed
about the international rules of war stated at the Geneva
Convention. The rules state that a prisoner must be treated
humanely, and has the right to adequate clothing, food,
shelter, and medical care. A POW is required to honestly
give the enemy his name, rank, and serial number, and

that is all. The U.S. Military Code of Conduct states what is expected of a prisoner of war.

Article 4 says, "If I become a prisoner of war, I will keep faith with my fellow prisoners. I will give no information or take part in any action which might be harmful to my comrades. If I am senior, I will take command. If not, I will obey the lawful orders of those appointed over me and will back them up in every way."

Article 5 says, "When questioned, should I become a prisoner of war, I am required to give name, rank, service number, and date of birth. I will evade answering further questions to the utmost of my ability. I will make no oral or written statements disloyal to my country and its allies or harmful to their cause." (U.S. Military Code of Conduct posted on Web site http://usmilitary.about.com)

In other words, we could talk ourselves out of a situation as long as we did not endanger our government's mission. We were on our own, and very much alone.

In my case, the silk map scarf became a very interesting item. The whole concept of the silk map scarf was fine, but if you are going to make use of the map, you must first evade the enemy for a chance to run for it. In my particular case, I was sighted all the way down and surrounded with firepower upon landing. I assume that my captors thought that the scarf had important intelligence for their

German friends. To that end, they started asking me to indicate on the map where various Allied airfields, etc. were located. By this time, having honestly given them my name, rank, and serial number, I decided that was the only truth they were going to get from me, and let the chips fall where they may. To answer their questions about the map, I would point out some of the most outlandish and false locations which I could dream up. To this day, I never found out whether they actually tried to pass that information on, but at least they finally gave up on the questions and put me in solitary confinement. At least they did not beat me, thinking that solitary would be enough at this point, I guess.

My life in this Budapest civil prison was not a pleasant one, with thin cabbage soup being my main source of food. To even get this, I was forced to pick the bowl up off the floor while a prison guard watched and laughed. My only satisfaction at this point was to curse this guy and trust he did not understand English. Since I was not the only inmate here—although we were not allowed to see each other—we did communicate some through the stone wall by tapping out the Morse code to each other. By this we did learn a little bit about each other. To pass the time, I made a deck of playing cards out of paper. I played solitaire by the hours. The big problem here was the bombings that often took place and were quite scary. We wished the bombers luck because we knew that they were "our guys" up there doing the bombing—Americans in the day-time and the British at night. The air raids were worrisome because our only defense was to get as close to a door-way arch as we could since they were stronger than the regular walls.

After 11 days of this, we were finally taken to what they called the marshalling yards where the trains were. The train was not as you envision it today—it was a small boxcar designed to hold 40 men or 8 horses. We were in a group of far more than 40, however we were all crammed into the car with no amenities. Although we did not know it at the time, we were headed for Sagan, Germany, loca-tion of Stalag Luft III, a permanent prisoner of war camp for English and American air corps personnel, and my home for the next several months.

LIEUT. GATEWOOD REPORTED MISSING OVER AUSTRIA

*Second Lieut. Vernon L. Gatewood has been reported miss-
ing in action over Austria since Sept. 10. War Department
telegrams conveying the message were received late Thurs-
day by his wife, the former Norma Jean Barth....*

—*Marietta Times*, September 22, 1944
Page 1, Column 4

CHAPTER 5
NEXT OF KIN

Fortunately, there was pretty good communication between the military and families during such a stressful time. I'm sure that everyone wanted to know more, but you can see from these letters that the government was trying to inform and explain the situation as best it could. Your grandmother had clipped a helpful article out of the newspaper in the fall of 1944 that tells families the military procedures for POW reporting. It is entitled "How Next of Kin Get Word," and in part, here is what it says:

As of October 1, 1944, there were some 55,000 U.S. soldiers, sailors and marines known to be prisoners of the German or Japanese. There were, in addition, some 58,000 reported missing....Article 77 of the Geneva Convention governs treatment of prisoners and requires that each of the ratifying powers [of the rules of the Geneva Convention] set up a Prisoner of War Information Bureau....

Before a man can be reported a prisoner of war, he must first be reported missing in action....A man doesn't become prisoner of war until he is so reported by the nation that captured him or by direct communication in the form of a capture card received from the prisoner himself, addressed to his next of kin. Ordinarily, however, the first word the next of kin will get is a telegram from the War Department saying that the man is missing in action. As soon as a man is captured, the enemy obtains from him such information as his name, rank, serial number, home address and next of kin. This information is sent by the enemy authorities to the International Red Cross. From the IRC at Geneva will come to the War Department an initial cable giving a list of newly reported prisoners by name, rank and serial number. From this list the Prisoner of War Information Bureau notifies the next of kin, giving the relative the first news that the man previously reported as missing in action is now a prisoner of war.

The Provost Marshal General's Office follows up the initial [telegram] with a letter to the next of kin, explaining how and where he may be communicated with. From 30 to 90 days later there will come a second cable...confirming names and numbers and specifying the prisoner of war camp to which each man has been assigned.

A second letter now goes out to the next of kin, relaying this new information and enclosing full mailing instructions and labels for mailing out parcels and tobacco. And in the Prisoner of War Information Bureau the case now becomes a record...so that the bureau has instantly available records on every individual....An index [of the records] is made out in duplicate. One copy stays in Washington, the other goes to General Eisenhower's headquarters, so that when the armies move into Germany, U.S. forces will know just what prisoners have to be accounted for, and where they are.

By Peter Edson, *Marietta Times*,
October 27, 1944, page 4.

This article pretty much explained the letters and telegrams that your grandmother got. So you see, the government's process of getting information to families was quite organized and efficient. Soon after I was shot down, word reached home by way of the MIA telegram to your grandmother:

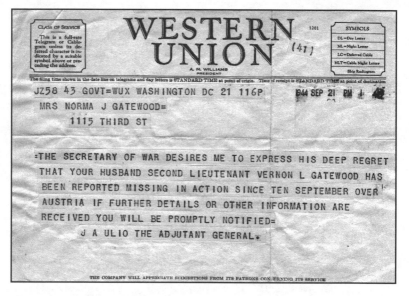

September 21, 1944, "Missing in Action" telegram from the adjutant general, Major General J. A. Ulio, to Mrs. Norma Gatewood

A more personal letter from General Ulio followed a few days later (see page 45).

Then another letter, this time from the Fifteenth Air Force's Major General N. F. Twining, arrived in October with more details about the mission (see page 46).

And then in November, word came in another telegram that I was a POW in Germany (see page 47).

WAR DEPARTMENT
THE ADJUTANT GENERAL'S OFFICE
WASHINGTON 25, D. C.

IN REPLY REFER TO:

AG 201 Gatewood, Vernon L.
   PC-N NAT226

23 September 1944

Mrs. Norma J. Gatewood
1115 3rd Street
Marietta, Ohio

Dear Mrs. Gatewood:

This letter is to confirm my recent telegram in which you were regretfully informed that your husband, Second Lieutenant Vernon L. Gatewood, O717885, Air Corps, has been reported missing in action over Austria since 10 September 1944.

I know that added distress is caused by failure to receive more information or details. Therefore, I wish to assure you that at any time additional information is received it will be transmitted to you without delay, and, if in the meantime no additional information is received, I will again communicate with you at the expiration of three months. Also, it is the policy of the Commanding General of the Army Air Forces upon receipt of the "Missing Air Crew Report" to convey to you any details that might be contained in that report.

The term "missing in action" is used only to indicate that the whereabouts or status of an individual is not immediately known. It is not intended to convey the impression that the case is closed. I wish to emphasize that every effort is exerted continuously to clear up the status of our personnel. Under war conditions this is a difficult task as you must readily realize. Experience has shown that many persons reported missing in action are subsequently reported as prisoners of war, but as this information is furnished by countries with which we are at war, the War Department is helpless to expedite such reports. However, in order to relieve financial worry, Congress has enacted legislation which continues in force the pay, allowances and allotments to dependents of personnel being carried in a missing status.

Permit me to extend to you my heartfelt sympathy during this period of uncertainty.

Sincerely yours,

J. A. ULIO
Major General,
The Adjutant General.

September 23, 1944, letter to Mrs. Norma Gatewood explaining meaning of term "missing in action"

19 October 1944

Mrs. Norma Jean Gatewood
1115 Third Street
Marietta, Ohio

Dear Mrs. Gatewood:

Your husband, Second Lieutenant Vernon L. Gatewood, O-717885, was the bombardier aboard one of our Liberators that took part in a bombing mission to Vienna, Austria, on September 10, 1944. His plane failed to return to its base and since that date he has been listed as missing in action.

Unfortunately, the extent of our knowledge is that Vernon's plane was lost because of damage by a burst of flak over the target. The bomber went down in the general vicinity of the objective. It was reported that all ten of the crew bailed out before the plane passed from view. I can well understand your desire for additional news but we can offer nothing beyond those details given above. You can rest assured that the War Department will notify you as soon as more definite information is forthcoming.

Your husband has displayed many of the qualities which make an excellent combat man. For his courage, devotion to duty, and willingness to face extreme physical hardships, he has been awarded the Air Medal.

Very sincerely yours,

N. F. TWINING
Major General, USA
Commanding

October 19, 1944, letter to Mrs. Norma Gatewood detailing mission on which Lieutenant Gatewood's plane was lost

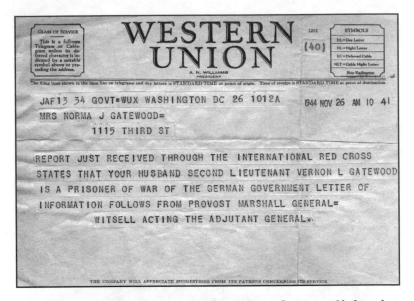

November 26, 1944, telegram to Mrs. Norma Gatewood informing of Lieutenant Gatewood's status as German prisoner of war

A letter from the Prisoner of War Information Bureau, Headquarters Army Service Forces, followed in early January with information on how to write to me (see page 48).

The International Red Cross was another method of communication; it was the official contact between families and prisoners of war. The Rules of the Geneva Convention also state that POWs have the right to send and receive family messages. Families in the States contacted the Red Cross for information on how to send packages and letters to POWs and in general to find out any news regarding POWs. You'll see where I mention that in some of my letters to your grandma.

1 January 1945

RE: 2nd Lt. Vernon L. Gatewood,
     United States Prisoner of War #7956,
     Stalag Luft 3, Germany.

Mrs. Norma J. Gatewood,
  1115 Third Street,
    Marietta, Ohio;

Dear Mrs. Gatewood:

      The Provost Marshal General has directed me to in-
form you further regarding the above-named prisoner of war.

      Information has been received which indicates that
his prisoner of war number is 7956. It is suggested that
you use this number when addressing future correspondence to
him.

      Sincerely yours,

      Howard F. Bresee

      Howard F. Bresee,
    Colonel, C.M.P., Director,
Prisoner of War Information Bureau.

January 1, 1945, letter from Colonel Howard F. Bresee, Army
Headquarters, Prisoner of War Information Bureau, telling how
to write to Lieutenant Gatewood

Despite the many letters and packages your grand-mother sent to me, I never got a one. Fortunately, she got mine, and she kept them. Our mail allotment allowed us to write three letters and four cards per month. She must have been so relieved to hear from me—I just wish I could have received something from her. In most of my letters to her I told her that I was fine and to keep her chin up, how I passed the time and that I was thinking of her. I also asked her to send supplies like cigarettes, chocolate, flour, baking powder, powdered and dried foods, vitamins, brown sugar, nuts, spices, and clothes. We really were hurting for supplies, but we couldn't say how bad we really were, because the Germans would censor it out. There is a line in one of my letters that is blackened out, or censored.

I wonder what happened to all those letters and pack-ages. We did get Red Cross packages at POW camp—at the beginning, one per week, then it went to one-half per week. Stories were going around that the packages from home and some of the Red Cross packages that we were supposed to get were actually going to the German troops on the battlefront now. Food was scarce for everyone—including the German military. Another story was that a lot of the letters from home were just thrown away and not delivered to the POWs.

Let me explain a little bit about the German words on these fold-up letters and postcards that I sent to your grandmother. The German word for prisoners of war was *"Kriegsgefangene,"* and *"Kriegsgefangenenpost"* was prisoner of war mail. My *"Gefangenennummer,"* or prisoner number, was 7956, and we were called *"Kriegies"* for short. So I was *Kriegie* #7956.

Note the German words, postmarks, and U.S. Censor stamps on the outsides of the letters and cards. Here's my first letter home. I'll read it to you because the pencil writing is so faint.

> Darling, my number is 7956,   Sept. 26, 1944
>   I know how you must have been worrying about me, but I want to tell you I am safe. Our whole crew got out allright. Kahn is with me here and Rinschler and Kelley [*sic*] should be on the way. I have seen Bob Williams for a few seconds....Do not worry as I will make out OK and see you soon when we can take up our normal lives again....Tell everyone hello and not to worry. I only hope you get this. We are all optimistic here, and are making out OK on the food. Get details on how to write from Red Cross. Write. I love you, Vernon

Knowing that she was worried about me and I was not getting any correspondence from her to tell me that she was getting my mail, on October 16, 1944, I wrote a letter (see page 52).

Front address sides of POW postcard *(Postkarte)* and letter *(Kriegsgefangenenpost)* from Lieutenant Gatewood

Darling, as I used to say; here Oct 16, 1944 is your hubby again, and loving you more and more each day I am away from you. Knowing you are waiting makes it so much easier here. We are treated O.K. here and have a lot of spare time on our hands. I've done a lot of reading, and am able to get some cigarettes. I hope it will be over in the not too far future, mommie, and we will again show people who the two most happily married people are, won't we? I wish I could give you details of my interesting, if not too pleasant experiences in the past month. I have many many things to be thankful for though. Use the address on this envelope to send mail to me, darling. My allotments should keep coming to you, and my pay is being held also, but the Red Cross will give you all that information.

Give my love to both families, darling, and just be patient and we will soon be together again. Be good, and keep building those castles in the air. I only hope you find out soon that I am a prisoner, so you won't worry too much. I am writing my mother today also. I have so much to say to you, darling our celebration will come. Vernon.

October 16, 1944, POW letter to Mrs. Norma Gatewood

Fortunately, the mail, if not TO us, then FROM us must have been pretty efficient. Here's my November 30, 1944, letter to her:

> Darling—As I write this, we are preparing to celebrate our Thanksgiving, that is to the best of our abilities and supplies....Have you received any of my letters yet? Write and let me know how you are passing the time....I have been feeling OK, except for what heat rash which won't go away. I haven't been doing much except reading and walking, as space will allow....Hello to all, send all food and cigarettes you can. Weather is really chilly here. Be good, sweet, and don't get discouraged and love—Vernon.

We often would inspect the seams of our clothes for lice—maybe that's why I had a "heat rash." We must have been pretty undernourished and not in the best of health. In my December 30, 1944, letter, I mentioned about having to do some cooking, and said that "...*even here old man KP is present, although supplies and equipment are limited." The* next line is blackened out or censored. Things were pretty tough, but we weren't able to say much about it in our letters.

Despite the tone of frustration and longing in my letters, they must have been a source of hope for your grandmother.

We had things to do and dreams to fulfill. These letters must have been what kept her going while I was a POW, just as her picture kept *me* going.

She kept these letters for all these years, and just having them reminded us of the hardships and the hopes we had at that time of our young lives. Our hopes and dreams *have* become realities—professionally and personally. Today, our family is the most important thing to us, and for that reason, we think it is time to pass the keeping of this part of the Gatewood family history on to you. Besides the hardships endured, remember what these letters represent to us—love of family, hope for the future, and the painful longing for freedom so our dreams of family and future could be realized.

If we ever get out of here, would you like one of my pictures?

—Floyd H. Greene, Jr. graphic artist and Sagan POW

CHAPTER 6
STALAG LUFT III—SAGAN

When our train arrived at Stalag Luft III—Sagan, we were herded off the railroad cars and marched into camp. A moment that I'll never forget was when we were marched through the several barbed wire gates to the various compounds, and to my great surprise I saw a personal friend, Captain Bob Williams from my hometown of Marietta, Ohio! Bob had been shot down much earlier as a pilot of a P-38 fighter plane flying out of Africa. I was so surprised and pleased that I fell out of rank and walked over to greet him. This was a great mistake on my part. The German guards let me know under no uncertain terms that breaking rank was just not done and it could lead me into further trouble if I didn't mend my ways. What a great way to start out my stay.

I was in West Compound of Stalag Luft III—there were four compounds for the four directions of the compass. In

German POW camps, officers were separated from enlisted men, so this camp was primarily for officers. There
were 15–20 barracks or long dormitory-like buildings in
each compound. Each barracks had several rooms—each
room was for eight to ten men. There were bunk beds
stacked three high and with straw-stuffed tick mattresses.
As I recall, we had one U.S. Army blanket each. As winter
approached, we slept in our clothes to gain whatever additional body heat we could. Our barracks had one central
wood burning stove from which we gained minor heat and
it was a cooking surface. The job of cooking was shared
by us all—we took turns preparing any food that managed
to come our way. It was here that I learned about blood
sausage, a horrible link thing that if you tried to heat it to
eat it, it would try to revert back to blood consistency. Even
in my state of hunger, I could never eat it. I think that we
were also fed some horse meat, which I did manage to
eat since we forced ourselves to not think deeply about it.
We were given a dark-brown bread that we swore was
part sawdust. When we cut it, it smelled like we were cutting a board in two, and it tasted about the same. We all
had dreams that we would share with each other, and the
most vivid ones were of food—especially chocolate. We
would dream of eating the richest, sweetest, largest serv-
ings you could possibly imagine. Some guys even wrote
up actual menus of meals that they planned to eat when
liberated.

According to the Geneva Convention, each prisoner was to receive one Red Cross parcel a week. Each parcel held such items as powdered milk cans, Spam cans, English crackers, a kind of semi-chocolate thing called a "D-Bar"—I don't remember what the "D" stood for—and a few other items. First, in order to prevent the prisoners' hoarding items for a possible escape try, the Germans would punch holes in lids of all canned items, therefore limiting the time the item would be edible. Secondly, since the war was at a point where the supply and delivery of the parcels were so difficult, the ration of the one parcel per prisoner per week was arbitrarily cut to one-half parcel per prisoner per week by the time I got to Sagan. To make the best of this situation, it was decided that we would form two-party partnerships to divide what we were given. As you might guess, this led to some interesting situations. It was decided that it would be fairest if one of us divided up the food, and the other decided what half he wanted. This would alternate daily, so that one day you would be the divider, and the next day you would be the chooser. In this hungry state, this led to some very careful measuring and choosing. It was a very serious business to both parties. We spent hours making sure that the division was even.

The Stalag Luft camps were staffed by German *Luftwaffe*—German Air Force—and members of the German *Abwehr* or home guard—sort of like our National

Guard, probably. Despite the German staffing, each compound had a commandant or senior American officer who
was in charge. He was a prisoner who had been at the
camp long enough to gain seniority. Our commandant was
a career military man, Colonel Darr Alkire, and he really
helped us through our ordeal. He was a tough, no non-
sense sort of a guy who maintained military order even in
dealing with the Germans. In conferences with German
officers, he didn't back down on anything. He stood up for
us and that helped our morale.

As identification, we were issued a two-part metal dog
tag that we had to wear all the time. This POW dog tag
had abbreviations for the camp name and number and my
POW number. On mine was stamped the number "7956."
One of the morbid things about the dog tag was that in the
case of death, the dog tag was broken in half—one half for
the record-keeping, one to remain with the body. I still have
mine—it's intact and I still carry it in my wallet. If you'll
remember, the first time I flew to visit you in Virginia, I set
off the security/metal detector at the airport with it!

Another piece of ID was a POW identification card
that the Germans kept in a box. When we were called to
line up for *der Appell*—roll call, they looked at us and looked
at the cards and our pictures to see if we all were there.
Sometimes to punish us, or just for harassment, they would

make us stand out there for hours. They kept our cards in a box in the commanding officer's area, and after liberation, we rushed in and took our cards as souvenirs. You can see that my card has my picture on it and spaces for name, POW number, rank, service number, nationality, and location in camp —*"Baracke"*—barracks—and *"Raum"*—room.

Lieutenant Gatewood's prisoner of war identification card

The camp at Sagan was pretty well established and it was rather organized—even as to the certain approved duties that inmates performed. One of these happened to be what we called the "ACCO," our kind of banking operation. The medium of exchange was a cigarette that held great value since money was neither present nor useful. For example, maybe an extra jar of jam that someone had been keeping could be "bought" with a few cigarettes. It turned out that my friend, Captain Bob Williams, due to his seniority at the camp had become an official of ACCO. He did not smoke, which led me to receive many of his cigarettes that I deposited in the ACCO and eventually became somewhat wealthy at the bank.

A little German language information might be helpful at this time. Prisoner of War Camps were called *Stalags* from the German *Stammlager,* meaning main camp. They were named *Stalag Luft* for those prisoners who were airmen, *Luft* meaning air. There were other designations for camps with other personnel such as *Marlag,* a prison camp for sailors; *Dulag Luft* was a transit camp for airmen; and *Milag* was a military camp.

There were over two hundred POW camps across Germany and its occupied countries, each housing many POWs from England, United States, Yugoslavia, Poland, and France.

Stalag Luft III was near the town of Sagan, Germany—now in the town of Zagan, Poland—and about one hundred fifty miles southeast of Berlin. Our camp, Stalag Luft III—Sagan, had about ten thousand prisoners at the height of its operation. Incidentally, this camp became famous due to the "The Great Escape" of March 1944 in which 80 Allied prisoners escaped from the camp, having dug a tunnel to beyond the fences. In the 1960s there was a movie based on this famous attempt. Most of the 80 men were killed by the Germans during the escape, but 15 made it to Allied lines. This happened much before my time there, and we were ordered to NOT attempt any escapes. It was beginning to look like we were gaining on the Germans at this time of the war, even though men were still dying every day.

The days and weeks at Sagan continued as a mix of despair, hunger, and dreams of rich foods. We were able to walk around the inside perimeter of the compound that was first bordered by a low wire called a "trip wire." If the trip wire was touched, it would signal one of the watch towers where some German guards were. Not good. Next was a bare area bordered by a high barbed wire fence, then a walk area where the German guards and their dogs patrolled. Finally another high barbed wire fence, beyond which I suppose was freedom, who knows. After the war, we were told that only a few of the dogs were actually trained as watch dogs; however, just their presence and their being led by a guard convinced us. Incidentally, those guard dogs were let loose inside our camp area at night to discourage any visitation between barracks.

We did do some reading from a limited library of sorts that had been started by other prisoners. During the day, we could walk outside our barracks, around the compound, and go check out a book in the small library. Sometimes we numbered up to 20 to a room, and had little to do. Often there was quite a bit of arguing. I recall one particular incident that actually led to a fist fight. One of our roommates was a tall guy named Tex who somehow managed to have a wrist watch. This made him a sort of top dog since we all would check with him as to the time of day. I now see that it really did not matter much anyhow, since we had no place to go. Tex was cranky about his position as timekeeper and did not like to be asked too often about what time it was. On one particular day, one of our guys kept asking about the time over and over again in a very short period of time. Tex got mad about this, told the guy to stop "or else!" The guy did not stop, so Tex proceeded to flail away at the offender. We pulled them apart before one of the "goons"—German guards—showed up, but at least this caused the rest of us to ease up on how often we checked the time.

There were several forms of diversion besides reading and walking, and one particular POW named Floyd Greene spent his time doing paintings. He came into our barracks once showing us some of his art. They were amazing. He had several versions of this graphic artwork

that showed a montage representing insignia and perti-
nent images of servicemen. He had drawn the images and
"painted" them using whatever pigments or stains he could
find in camp—shoe polish, food juices, charcoal maybe.
He had one for pilots/copilots, one for navigators, and one
for bombardiers. He said, "If we ever get out of here, would
you like one of my pictures?" I was really impressed with
the quality and the thought that went into his works, so I
signed up—gave him my name and address. After the war,
he contacted me; I bought one of his prints. I'm sending a
color copy of it for you to see. You might remember that
the original is framed on our "Memory Wall" at home here.

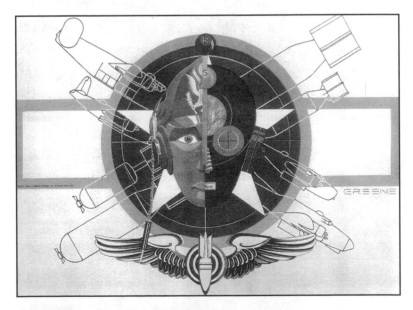

Floyd H. Greene's bombardier graphic artwork

I thought that you might like to know what the parts mean, so I'll describe it for you.

First of all, you'll see that the graphic has a face superimposed over a military insignia. The red circle and horizontal box with the five-pointed star in the background is the Army Air Corps insignia. Below the face, you'll see bombardier wings with a bomb in the center. Extending out at angles from the face and insignia are outlines of different planes—a B-24, B-17, B-26, and A-20—and then bombs from the other angles. The face has a human side and a mechanical side. The human side has the headphone and a cord extending down from it. This was the connection to our intercom system so we could listen to other members of the crew. We talked through a "throat mike" that was connected to the intercom system. Remember, it was noisy up there, so that was the only way we could hear each other.

The mechanical side has symbols for the tools of the bombardier. The "forehead" is a leveling mechanism that used an air bubble in a fluid for making sure the plane was level both ways before dropping the bombs. The "eye" is the cross hairs I looked through for sighting the targets. The "ear" is a hand-sized control knob used to maneuver the plane upon preparing to drop the bombs. These are all parts of the top-secret Norden bombsight that I used. The "nose" is a part of an oxygen tube, the mouth is an off/on toggle switch that activated the bomb sight, and the red knob at the top of the forehead is the salvo knob. When we needed or wanted to drop all the bombs at once, we pulled the salvo release knob.

It is so accurate and such a symbolic piece. Mr. Greene also made drawings of a navigator and another of a pilot—the background was the same on the others, but the details were specific to those other two positions on the bomber. I don't know whether my print has any real value, but it is so important to me. It reminds me how we were trained and outfitted for our job. It represents the experiences and hardships we endured in our fight for freedom.

I lost track of Floyd Greene after I bought the print and I haven't been able to locate him despite lots of letters and calls to many "Greenes" across the country. Maybe someday I'll find him.

At his 4:30 staff meeting in Berlin on the afternoon of January 27, 1945, Adolf Hitler issued the order to evacuate Stalag Luft 3....The order triggered an ordeal and an adventure that would be frozen for life into the psyches of every Kriegie *who survived it.*

—From the *Kriegie Klarion*,
the Stalag Luft III—Sagan POW newsletter
50th Anniversary Issue
January 1995

CHAPTER 7
THE *KRIEGIE* MARCH

In January 1945, Hitler was fearful that the thousands of airmen at our camp would be liberated by the Russian army that was approaching quickly from the east. Preparations for our evacuation were all very rushed. We put on what clothes we could find and lined up to be counted. Because of the serious mood of the guards and the disorganized bunch of several thousand prisoners, I'm sure the count was not very accurate. To utilize the food we had, everyone ate as much as they could—we gorged ourselves. Finally, at about 12:30 A.M., the West Compound POWs started our historic march.

66

As we moved out, the weather conditions were terrible, with about six inches of snow on the ground and a biting wind blowing. We marched for over 24 hours with one four-hour stop somewhere in between, where we were allowed to find barns and stables or whatsoever shelter we were lucky enough to find. It was here that several of us found out that if we would burrow into a pile of hay and manure, we could gain some warmth. That was *very* welcome in spite of the odor. At this point, who cared? We moved on, and the next night we stayed in a large concrete pipe plant which contained some heat from the process of manufacturing the pipe. I was told later that this plant was in a town called Muskau, and we had marched about 33 miles since Sagan.

During these marches I did several very, very foolish things, which I later regretted. To start the march, I had been able to get an American army wool overcoat which was quite long and warm. As I became more and more exhausted from the marching, I cut the bottom part of the coat off to decrease the weight. Bad, bad mistake. Due to the weight, if you can imagine this, also I threw away a notebook that I was keeping as sort of a diary. In this diary were many names of my fellow prisoners with whom I had hoped to remain in contact if we ever survived. Brief entries about my POW experiences were also in this 5 x 7 notebook. Years later, I realized that this was my most valuable asset and that I could never recreate that list. I wish I had it now so I could read from it for you. Another thing that I did due to the cold, snow, ice, and my fatigue— I bound my GI shoes in cloth rags thinking that this would allow me to walk better. What actually happened was that the bindings soon froze to the point where I could not bend my ankles properly enough to walk. I can see it right now— *crazy*—clumping along like Frankenstein! After realizing that this was working against me, I cut the bindings off at my earliest opportunity.

We must have been quite a sight. I heard later that our marching line extended for 20 miles. The guards were constantly herding us, yelling at us, and shooting over our heads. They kept shooting over our heads as a power threat. They wanted to let us know that they meant business despite the fact that we outnumbered them. Again, these were not first line or hard core soldiers, but "home guard types." The best of the German military personnel was on the battlefront, so this group of guards was maybe retired or in part-time military service. A lot of them were over age to be soldiering and perhaps they were called in from the reserve ranks to guard this massive movement.

One of the strangest things that happened not only to me but to many others, was that after marching for so many hours, we would hallucinate and imagine that we could see lights of towns that did not really exist. By that point I had lost track of all time and distance, but I later found out that we had walked about 60 miles from Sagan. At that location, we were herded again into the famous "40 and 8" train cars in a town called Spremburg. Conditions were pretty bad. We did not have room to either sit or lie down; we were crammed into these boxcars pretty tightly. We would take turns sitting down. Many of the prisoners were sick and had diarrhea *and* we had no sanitation. It began to smell like one great big toilet in there. This phase led us into our next camp at Nürnberg. We never knew how long we were going to be somewhere, where we were going, or how long we were going to be marching.

Somehow, information got back home about the Russians approaching Sagan. Your grandma saved a little article from the newspaper that told how three Marietta families (one being my family, of course) were waiting for more news from Sagan. They were hoping that their airmen, who were POWs there, had been freed by the Russians, or moved to another camp by the Germans as the Russians approached Sagan.

Maybe my February 18, 1945, letter to your grandma says it best. I must have been in Nürnberg after our first leg of what was coming to be called "the death march" when I wrote this.

We have now changed location as you may possibly know when you receive this. We had quite a journey and I want to let you know I made it OK and in as good a shape as possible. We hope peace comes soon. Love to all. I have received no mail or word from you, but hope you have been getting word from me....Love, Gate

By then we had either walked or ridden about two hundred fifty miles—in snowy, cold January. I've often thought that this experience of marching in the snow and cold of winter made me cold-natured. You know that I really do hate the snow and I always have trouble getting or staying warm in the winter. Could it be that this extended period of being cold all the time continues to affect me?

President Roosevelt is Dead; Truman To Continue Policies;
9th Crosses Elbe, Nears Berlin

—*The New York Times* headline
Friday, April 13, 1945

CHAPTER 8
NÜRNBERG, MOOSBURG, AND LIBERATION

Conditions at Nürnberg were certainly no improvement over Sagan—just the opposite. By that time of the war, the Germans were badly organized, if at all, and our welfare was no longer on their minds. They were losing the war and they didn't know what to do with us. We were in tents, no Red Cross parcels did we see, and our hygiene consisted of a water faucet in an open area of the compound. Camp was very overcrowded, sanitation was practically nil with insufficient toilet facilities, food was scarce and of poor quality. We had a "joke" that the soup they gave us was 50 percent peas and 50 percent bugs. I remember one time that one of us was preparing our meager food allotment and he began to peel the potatoes. Another POW yelled at him, "Don't do that, you're wasting half the potato!" Air raids became a routine part of our lives. We headed for the slit trenches so often that some of the prisoners just spent the rest of many nights there. I lost track of the time we spent there, but at least the weather was starting to moderate somewhat.

Finally one day we were told that we were about to march again. By now the Germans could see the end of the war, and they were not about to give us up. At least we found out that we were bound for Moosburg for Stalag VII A. So off we went again.

As a matter of "comfort" and survival, I did a couple of things that helped me. One thing I did was I tried to keep a pair of clean socks in reserve. I remember washing them and then carrying them on my stomach the next day so they could dry. When we were given the opportunity, we helped ourselves to any foodstuffs in farmhouses along the way. With so many prisoners, we were able to wander off the march line sometimes. I remember getting some fresh eggs and a sausage from a farmhouse one time. I kept the sausage in my jacket pocket and nibbled on it from time to time on the march. I'll show you the jacket sometime and you can see the stain that remains on the right pocket.

In that march we could detect a slight relaxing in the efforts of the guards, which led us to become even more aggressive in our movements. Once again, several of us broke out of our marching column and went into another nearby farmhouse. We told the farmer and his family that the Russians were just one day behind us and that they should feed us and make it easier on themselves for when the Russians arrived. Russia was one of our Allies, but she was not very favored or thought of very highly by us. The Germans certainly were afraid of the Russians and their coarse, militant ways. We were rather threatening to the farmer, and we may not have been in a very good position to do that, but we did. Our threats were of course, not true, but it did get us some bread and eggs. We were preparing this in the farmer's kitchen until we were caught by the mayor of whatever small hamlet we were near. He was very "put out" to say the least, and he got the guards to put us back in line—that massive column of marchers.

Despite these diversions, our morale was low and we were all so miserable with the cold and the duration of the march. We didn't know how much longer it was going to be before we got to Moosburg. We were able to draw inspiration from one incident. Along the way, we saw one of our P-38 fighter planes flying with only one of its two engines functioning. He was in very bad shape and flying pretty low. Flying beside this crippled plane was his "wingman flying protection." The "wingman" was another fighter plane that flew beside a disabled plane and tried to get him back to home base. This "wingman" gave the plane in trouble an escort and gave him much needed moral support. It was an emotional and inspiring moment for us all—we felt that if HE could make it, so could we.

One date on the march stands out in my mind—April 12. We don't know how "the word" got to the line of marchers, but word was passed up by mouth from one person to another: President Roosevelt had died. The amazing thing about it was that at that point in our lives, we thought that President Roosevelt, our commander in chief, would be there forever. He had just been reelected to his fourth term, and we had known no one else as the leader of our country. We were devastated.

This news was not only sad to us from the standpoint of personal loss, but we thought that since our leader had passed away, the war would continue much longer. We had been hearing rumors of "peace will come soon" and "the war is winding down," so the news about Roosevelt's death made us very discouraged. Also, I doubt that very many of us knew much about our new president, Harry Truman. A lot of us might not have even recognized the name at that time. I do not know how far we marched on that particular day; however, I do recall that when we were finally allowed to stop and rest, it was a very sad night indeed. The guards, who by now had also received the news, made us feel that since Roosevelt had died, we would be in *their* care for the rest of our lives. We've always believed that the German guards were trained to keep the POW morale at its very lowest ebb.

Finally, after an uncounted number of days and marching about one hundred more miles, we entered Stalag VII A at Moosburg. I later read in some of my POW newsletters that officers from Nürnberg—that would be my group—arrived on April 19. I also read that the Germans held about 110,000 Allied prisoners at Moosburg. This compound was similar to Sagan with guard towers, double barbed wire fences, and barracks. I don't remember very much about day-to-day activities at the camp since I was only there for a few weeks. I do remember that it was very crowded. Due to the overcrowding, men were sleeping not only in the three-tiered bunks, but on floors of barracks, on tables, and in tents outside. Thousands of POWs had been gathered here from other POW camps. With the massive numbers of prisoners here, things got even more unhealthy. At this camp we didn't even have a faucet for washing. Despite this lack of sanitation, we attempted to keep our appearances somewhat neat, and I remember cutting someone's hair with a pair of manicure scissors—the only ones we could find. We had white bread here—I don't know where it came from, but we hadn't had white bread since we were shot down. It was a welcome, fond memory of civilized American food.

Despite the bad conditions at Moosburg, rumors of our release were getting hotter each day. Hitler's Germany was being squeezed from the east by the Russians, who had Berlin under siege, and by the Allied forces invading and liberating from the north and west. Then on April 29, 1945, General George Patton's 14th Armored Division of the Third Army entered the camp, received the surrender of all Germans, and started the long procedures needed to get us repatriated. I will never forget the sight of General Patton himself standing upright in his Jeep, wearing his trademarks: shiny, shellacked, highly polished helmet and his two pearl-handled .45 side arms. He was an imposing sight as he was driven through the shouting, cheering, and now, EX-prisoner throng. During this time of jubilation, we ran into the camp office and got our POW cards as souvenirs. Although the war was not over yet, it was the beginning of the end of our ordeal.

Your grandmother received a telegram from General Ulio a few weeks later (see next page).

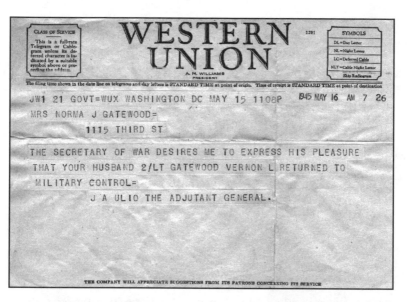

May 16, 1945, "Returned to military control" telegram from Adjutant General Ulio received by Mrs. Norma Gatewood

THE CHIEF OF STAFF OF THE ARMY DIRECTS ME TO INFORM YOU YOUR HUSBAND LT GATEWOOD VERNON L IS BEING RETURNED TO THE UNITED STATES WITHIN THE NEAR FUTURE AND WILL BE GIVEN AN OPPORTUNITY TO COMMUNICATE WITH YOU UPON ARRIVAL

J A ULIO THE ADJUTANT GENERAL
TELEGRAM TO MRS. NORMA J. GATEWOOD
May 21, 1945

Chapter 9
Passing on the Pursuit

After that liberation day, we were put on the big C-47 airplanes and taken to Camp Lucky Strike, one of the U.S. Army Camps near LaHavre on the northern coast of France. I remember flying over Paris and seeing the Eiffel Tower as we were evacuated from Germany. At Camp Lucky Strike we were catalogued, deloused, and medically examined and prepared to be discharged from the service. We were then put on troop transports and taken to Liverpool, England. At Liverpool, we were put on ships to take us back to the States. I weighed only 90 pounds at liberation; my pre-POW camp weight was around 145 pounds. On the ship home, the goal was to fatten us up and put our weight back on in a hurry. They fed us well—the mainstays in the menus were elbow macaroni, Spam, peanut butter, and Jell-O. We ate A LOT of Jell-O. I still like macaroni, Spam, and peanut butter, but I can leave the Jell-O alone.

It was an emotional moment when our ship sailed into New York Harbor and I saw the Statue of Liberty. I was overwhelmed. This statue was a symbol of the freedom that we had pursued for so long—first as men on a mission, second as POWs.

Our ship continued up the coast and docked in Boston. I called your grandmother—one of the things I remember telling her was that I really wanted some hot dogs and hamburgers! I was still thinking about all sorts of good food. I've forgotten the details here, but somehow I got on a train that took me to Parkersburg to meet her. The government had already planned our time together for a while, however. We were assigned quarters in a hotel in Miami Beach, Florida, and had sort of a rest and recuperation period. During that time, I had lots of debriefings about my experiences. I had to take lots of tests and answer lots of questions.

After a few days in Miami Beach, your grandmother went on back to Marietta and I had to go to Texas for final preparations to be separated from the service. When I was finishing up what I had to do in Texas I wrote another telegram to your grandmother saying,

1945 AUGUST 15
BE HERE TEN DAYS THEN OFF TO ATTERBURY
AND DISCHARGE GET READY FOR PLAIN MR
AND MRS....LETTER FOLLOWS LOVE VG

I was honorably discharged at Atterbury, Indiana, separation center on September 10, 1945—exactly a year after I was shot down. A lot had happened in that time. We were more than ready to begin our civilian lives as "plain Mr. and Mrs.," and so grateful that we could. There were so many who did not make it back to continue their private lives. We must remember them when we reap the benefits of their sacrifices.

You asked whether I got any medals. I've sent you my studio portrait that I had taken after I returned to Marietta.

You'll notice I do have some ribbons and medals on my jacket. The ribbon bars represent the more formal pin-on ornate medals that you keep in a box at home. One of the ribbons is blue and orange and has an oak cluster medal on it. This is the ribbon version of the air medal. The actual pin-on air medal itself is a medallion hanging from a triangular section of blue ribbon with thin stripes of orange

Portrait of Lieutenant Vernon L. "Gate" Gatewood—Fall 1945

and blue on the edges. Each airman got an air medal after completing so many missions. I was also awarded the European-African-Middle Eastern Service Medal. This "theater-of-war medal" is designated by a green, orange, and white ribbon bar with two stars. The colors denote the Southern Italy location of the European Theater in which I served. You'll also notice "my wings" in the portrait—the wings have a bomb in the center to signify that I was in the United States Army Air Force and trained as a bombardier. This is the same symbol that Floyd Greene put in that powerful painting he did in POW camp.

In 1988, the government sent me some papers to fill out regarding my POW status. I sent them in and was issued the POW medal. The ribbon bar of this medal is mostly black, edged with thin red, white, and black stripes. The design on the medallion is a spread eagle encircled with barbed wire, hanging from a black ribbon bordered with red, white, and black. This medal came as a surprise to me—I think that new legislation had been passed to honor veterans who had been POWs.

As somewhat of a civilian honor, I became a member of the Caterpillar Club. You probably won't find much information on it, but I'm enclosing my membership card that will help explain it to you. It's sort of a funny thing about something pretty serious. Membership is for only those whose lives were saved by using a silk parachute. One company, The Switlick Company, sent me the membership card, certificate, and lapel pins of the Caterpillar Club.

The logo of the Caterpillar Club is the silk moth caterpillar which spun silk fibers that were harvested and woven into fabric for parachutes. One of my pins has red eyes to signify that my plane went down in flames. When you come again, you can see my medals and pins, my stained jacket, and the framed print of my Caterpillar Club certificate on the Memory Wall.

This is to certify that
LT. VERNON L. GATEWOOD
Is a member of the Caterpillar Club whose life was spared the 10 day of September 1944 because of an emergency parachute jump from an aircraft. Membership certificate has been issued to the end that this safety medium in the art of flying may be futhered.
10-27-45

ISSUED   SECRETARY

Membership card presented by the Switlick Company to acknowledge Lieutenant Gatewood whose life was spared because of an emergency parachute jump from an aircraft

As I prepare these things for you, I'm looking at the Memory Wall here at home. There are lots of memories here—of family, holidays, and travels. All of these are possible because I was successful in returning safely. There were so many who were not so lucky. My prisoner of war experience was not a pleasant period of my life, but I must say that any recognition of the POW experience must also include gratitude to *all* members of all branches of armed forces who served and returned. Special prayers must go for those who served and did not return. We all made sacrifices, but some gave the supreme sacrifice of their lives for securing our freedoms. We must remember all of those who served and continue their pursuit whenever or wherever freedom is threatened.

So, here on this tape are the things I remember, along with some letters and things that I thought you'd like to see. You must remember that this story is being told some 50+ years after it happened, so I have to have a disclaimer. Some details might have eluded me, but this is what I remember to the best of my ability now. I *did* find it difficult to revisit these emotions and experiences. It was hard then, and it is hard now to talk about them. For so many years I tried to forget these difficult times in my life. Knowing that you wanted to know about my experiences helped me do it, though. Now you know what "The Good War" was about from my viewpoint and how it affected our family history.

Let me just say that the pursuit of freedom may be painful, but it *is* worth fighting for. The pursuit of freedom by those millions of military people in World War II determined our country's history and that of the world. Don't ever forget that these were hard-fought battles of sacrifice. I suppose that I'm trying to say that I'm "passing on the pursuit" to you. Be grateful for your freedom and never take it for granted. Maybe these mementos will remind you of the hard-fought freedoms that we now enjoy and encourage you to cherish them in years to come.

So, there you have it. There's probably more here than you bargained for! Looking forward to seeing you and the family in February. Maybe we can talk some more then. I vote for no snow and no Jell-O!

All my Love, Grandpa

* * * * *

Betsy pushed the STOP button on her tape player. She paused and reflected on the wealth of information that she had just heard and seen. With determination and newly found purpose and direction, she then ran downstairs to the computer. She couldn't wait to tell Grandpa's story. She was inspired, proud, and honored to know this important part of the Gatewood family history.

The words began to fly from her fingers as she started her assignment: *A World War II Bombardier's Pursuit of*

Freedom. She knew that this paper was going to earn her that "A"—but now the grade didn't seem so important. Grandpa had helped her learn world history in the most personal way. This history lesson would stay with her for a lifetime.

50 years later
Norma Jean and Vernon L. Gatewood—May 1992

Bibliography

Books

Ambrose, Stephen E., and C. L. Sulzberger. *American Heritage New History of World War II*. New York: Viking Press, 1997.

Burger, Leslie, and Debra L. Rahm. *Red Cross Red Crescent—When Help Can't Wait*. Minneapolis: Lerner Publications Company, 1996.

Byers, Roland O., ed. *Black Puff Polly and Other Flights to Eternity*. Moscow, Idaho: Pawpaw Press, 1991.

Childers, Thomas. *Wings of Morning: The Story of the Last American Bomber Shot Down Over Germany in World War II*. Reading, Mass.: Addison-Wesley Publishing Company, 1995.

Colby, C. B. *Bomber Parade: Headliners in Bomber Plane History*. New York: Coward-McCann, Inc., 1960.

Cubbins, William R. *The War of the Cottontails—Memoirs of a WW II Bomber Pilot*. Chapel Hill: Algonquin Books of Chapel Hill, 1989.

Davis, Larry. *B-24 Liberators in Action*. Carrollton, Tex.: Squadron/Signal Publications, Inc., 1987.

Gray, Ronald. *Hitler and the Germans.* Minneapolis, Minn.: Lear Publications Company, 1983.

Hoyt, Edwin P. *Hitler's War.* New York: McGraw-Hill Book Company, 1988.

Munson, Kenneth. *Fighters and Bombers of World War II: 1939–45.* New York: Exeter Books, 1969.

Sullivan, George. *Famous Air Force Bombers.* New York: Dodd, Mead and Company, 1985.

Time-Life Books, ed. *The American Story World War II.* Alexandria, Va.: Time-Life Books, 1997.

Time-Life Books, ed. *Decade of Triumph—The 40's.* Alexandria, Va.: Time-Life Books, 1999.

Web Sites

Aircraft nose art—http://www.bombergirl.com/noseart/noseart1.htm

"Cigarette Camps" in LaHavre, France—http://www.skylighters.org/special/cigcamps/cmplstrk.html

The Collings Foundation—http://www.collingsfoundation.org/index.html

The Cottontails Scrapbook—http://www.450thbg.com/HTiVL/index.html

German Prisoner of War Camps—http://www.geocities.com/plowwii/uk083_stalag_overview.htm

Heavybombers—http://www.heavybombers.com

Moosburg, Germany, Stalag VII POW camp—http:// www.moosburg.org/info/stalag/indeng.html

Ploesti missions—http://www.airforcehistory.hq.af.mil/soi/ ploesti.htm

Rod Powers—U.S. Military Guide (Military Code of Conduct)—http://www.usmilitary.about.com

Stalag Luft III POW camp information—http://www.B24.net/ pow/stalag3.htm

U.S. Air Force Museum—http://www.wpafb.af.mil/museum

INDEX

40 and 8 boxcars, 40, 69

ACCO (Prisoner of War camp banking operation), 59–60
Alkire, Colonel Darr, 58
Allies (U.S., Britain, France), 19, 39, 73, 76
Army Air Corps, 22, 64
Army Air Field assignments
  Big Spring Army Air Field, Texas, 14, 17
  Charleston Army Air Field, South Carolina, 17
  Keesler Field, Mississippi, 11–12
  Mitchell Field, New York, 17, 22
  Westover Field, Massachusetts, 14, 17
Aryan race, 19

B-24 "Liberator," aircraft, 21–22, 28, 64
  crew, 5, 16, 22, 50
  Davis wing, 25
  machine guns, 16–17, 24
bombardier, job and duties, 9, 13–14, 16–17, 22, 25–26, 64, 82
Bresee, Colonel Howard F., 48
Budapest, Hungary, 37, 39

Camp Lucky Strike, 78
Caterpillar Club, 82
Christy, Leonard, 9
cigarettes, 35, 59–60
commission, 14
Cottontails, 22

deferment, 9

democracy, 2, 8, 18–19
dictatorship, 18

electric suit, 25
enlistment, 9
ethnic cleansing, 19
everyone's war, 9, 19

flak *(Fliegerabwehrkanone)* (anti-aircraft gun), 21, 24–25, 28–29, 32
  suit (for protection), 24, 30, 32
flight instructor, 14, 21–22
forced march (*Kriegie* march), 66
  morale, 73, 75
  Nürnberg to Moosburg, 72
  Sagan to Nürnberg, 67–69
  stolen sausage, 72
freedom, 2–3, 7–9, 18, 20, 54, 65, 79, 84–85
freedom fighters, 2–3

Gatewood family history, 54, 84–85
Geneva Convention, 37, 42, 47, 57
Germans
  economic depression, 18
  as the enemy, 4, 14, 18–19, 22, 57–58, 69, 71–73
"Good War, The," 4, 7, 84
Great Escape, The (movie), 61
Greene, Floyd H., 55, 62, 65, 82
Greene graphic print, 62–63
Gyor, Hungary, 35

Hitler, Adolf, 18–19, 66, 76
humor in spite of war, 9, 31
Hungarian people, 34–37

immunizations, 14

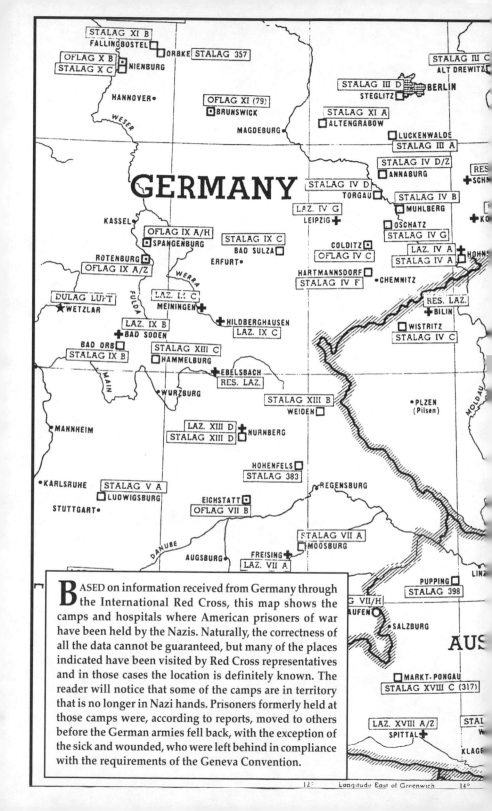

STALAG XI B
FALLINGBOSTEL
☐ ORBKE STALAG 357

OFLAG X B
STALAG X C ☐ NIENBURG

STALAG III C
ALT DREWITZ

STALAG III D ☐ BERLIN
STEGLITZ

HANNOVER •

OFLAG XI (79)
☐ BRUNSWICK

STALAG XI A
☐ ALTENGRABOW

WESER

MAGDEBURG •

☐ LUCKENWALDE
STALAG III A

GERMANY

STALAG IV D/Z
☐ ANNABURG

RES
SCHM

STALAG IV D
TORGAU ☐

STALAG IV B
☐ MUHLBERG

KO

KASSEL •

LAZ. IV G
LEIPZIG ✚

OSCHATZ
STALAG IV G

OFLAG IX A/H
☐ SPANGENBURG

STALAG IX C
BAD SULZA ☐

COLDITZ ☐
OFLAG IV C

LAZ. IV A
STALAG IV A ☐ HOHNS

ROTENBURG ☐
OFLAG IX A/Z

ERFURT •

HARTMANNSDORF ☐
STALAG IV F ☐

• CHEMNITZ

WERRA

DULAG LUFT
★ WETZLAR

FULDA

LAZ. IX C
MEININGEN ✚

RES. LAZ.
✚ BILIN

LAZ. IX B
✚ BAD SODEN

✚ HILDBERGHAUSEN
LAZ. IX C

☐ WISTRITZ
STALAG IV C

BAD ORB ☐
STALAG IX B

STALAG XIII C
☐ HAMMELBURG

MAIN

✚ EBELSBACH
RES. LAZ.

• WURZBURG

STALAG XIII B
WEIDEN ☐

• PLZEN
(Pilsen)

MOLDAU

• MANNHEIM

LAZ. XIII D
STALAG XIII D ✚ NURNBERG

• KARLSRUHE

STALAG V A
☐ LUDWIGSBURG

HOHENFELS ☐
STALAG 383

REGENSBURG

STUTTGART •

EICHSTATT ☐
OFLAG VII B

DANUBE

AUGSBURG •

FREISING ✚
LAZ. VII A

STALAG VII A
☐ MOOSBURG

PUPPING ☐
STALAG 398

LIN

G VII/H
AUFEN

• SALZBURG

AUS

☐ MARKT- PONGAU
STALAG XVIII C (317)

LAZ. XVIII A/Z
SPITTAL ✚

STAL
W

KLAGE

BASED on information received from Germany through the International Red Cross, this map shows the camps and hospitals where American prisoners of war have been held by the Nazis. Naturally, the correctness of all the data cannot be guaranteed, but many of the places indicated have been visited by Red Cross representatives and in those cases the location is definitely known. The reader will notice that some of the camps are in territory that is no longer in Nazi hands. Prisoners formerly held at those camps were, according to reports, moved to others before the German armies fell back, with the exception of the sick and wounded, who were left behind in compliance with the requirements of the Geneva Convention.

12°   Longitude East of Greenwich   14°